Issues in
Civilian Outplacement Strategies

Proceedings of a Workshop

Renae F. Broderick, Editor

Commission on Behavioral and Social Sciences and Education
National Research Council

NATIONAL ACADEMY PRESS
Washington, D.C. 1996

NOTICE: The project that is the subject of this report was approved by the Governing Board of the National Research Council, whose members are drawn from the councils of the National Academy of Sciences, the National Academy of Engineering, and the Institute of Medicine. The members of the committee responsible for the report were chosen for their special competences and with regard for appropriate balance.

This report has been reviewed by a group other than the authors according to procedures approved by a Report Review Committee consisting of members of the National Academy of Sciences, the National Academy of Engineering, and the Institute of Medicine.

This work is sponsored by the Office of the Deputy Assistant Secretary of Defense (Civilian Personnel and Policy) and funded under Defense Supply Services Contract No. DASW01-95-C-0139. The views, opinions, and findings contained in this report are those of the author(s) and should not be construed as an official Department of Defense position, policy, or decision, unless so designated by other official documentation.

Library of Congress Catalog Card Number 96-69970

International Standard Book Number 0-309-05544-X

Additional copies of this report are available from National Academy Press, 2101 Constitution Avenue, N.W., Box 285, Washington, D.C. 20055. Call 800-624-6242 or 202-334-3313 (in Washington Metropolitan Area). Order electronically via Internet at http://www.nap.edu.

Printed in the United States of America

COMMISSION ON BEHAVIORAL AND SOCIAL SCIENCES AND EDUCATION

Preface

Over the next 5 years, some 75 military bases in the continental United States will be closed. This is part of a larger picture of downsizing and defense conversion efforts brought about as a consequence of the collapse of the Soviet Union as a rival world power and of difficult budget realities closer to home. Reductions in the numbers of military personnel, already well under way, will bring the military to its lowest force levels since before the Korean War. Most of these reductions will be achieved in the form of lower recruiting goals and smaller numbers of accessions, although a significant number of career officers and enlisted personnel will also be affected.

The civilian workforce of the U.S. Department of Defense does not, like the uniformed one, depend on a base of constantly changing young people who serve for a term or two. Downsizing it cannot be accomplished by the relatively painless process of reducing the number of hires. Although the Department of Defense is pursuing all downsizing options, including early retirements, special leaves, and internal transfers, reductions must be accomplished largely by eliminating the jobs of people who have spent their careers supporting the military services. In addition, downsizing through base closings has a direct and concentrated impact on the communities in which the bases are located. In many communities, such as Charleston, South Carolina, the military is the dominant employer. California presents the example of a state suffering not just multiple base closures, but also severe cutbacks in the defense industry, a major source of high-salaried, high-technology jobs. Military installations in small communities throughout the South have encouraged the growth of a service infrastructure that, absent the military presence, the local economies may not be able to support. In all of these cases, the reemployment picture for civilians currently employed at the military bases is not strong; moreover, the impact of base closings will be felt more or less severely by the local economy.

For many employees, help in finding new jobs or training opportunities to make them more marketable is the key to mitigating the effects of base closings. The Office of the Deputy Assistant Secretary of Defense for Civilian Personnel Policy asked the National Academy of Sciences for assistance in understanding the range of outplacement issues and options available to them based on what has been learned in other settings, especially in the private sector.

In February 1996 the Commission on Behavioral and Social Sciences and Education of the National Research Council held a workshop to present existing research and best practices for employee outplacement. Participants included Department of Defense officials involved in developing outplacement policies, academics currently conducting related research, representatives from private industry directly involved in outplacement, and consultants specializing in this area. We gratefully acknowledge the support of Diane Disney, Deputy Assistant Secretary of Defense for Civilian Personnel Policy, and her staff.

We wish to thank Renae F. Broderick for her work in planning the workshop and drafting this proceedings. We are especially grateful to Carolyn Sax, staff of the Commission on Behavioral and Social Sciences and Education, who took on major responsibilities for organizing the workshop and preparing the manuscript. Finally, we are indebted to the workshop presenters and participants for their contributions to the success of the workshop.

John A. Swets, *Chair*
Commission on Behavioral and Social Sciences and Education

Alexandra K. Wigdor, *Director*
Division on Education, Labor, and Human Performance

Contents

Issues in

Civilian Outplacement Strategies

Proceedings of a Workshop

Introduction

Between September 1989 and September 1995, planned downsizing reduced the civilian workforce of the U.S. Department of Defense from over 1 million to just under 850,000. By the year 2001, this number will be reduced by another 119,000. As Deputy Assistant Secretary for Civilian Personnel Policy Diane Disney noted in her opening remarks, "The Department of Defense is undergoing a restructuring and downsizing that dwarfs what is going on in the private sector. Reductions in military personnel are, for all practical purposes, over; the civilian reduction is not. The good news is that we are two-thirds of the way through. The bad news is that we still have one-third to go."

This workshop was organized to generate creative ideas about outplacement for this "one-third to go." In particular, the Department of Defense wanted to bring together a group of private-sector executives to discuss outplacement practices that have been effective in helping their departing employees find new jobs. To add to the discussion, several scholars and professionals with experience in outplacement were asked to write research or practice summaries and participate in the workshop. The workshop format comprised two sessions: the first covered current research on outplacement, and the second covered industry outplacement experiences.

One of the workshop participants, Anne Messenger of Lockheed Martin, noted that there are many different names for the phenomenon of outplacement, often used interchangeably: reengineering, firing, downsizing, right sizing, unemployment, dislocation, layoffs, and outplacement. Ten years ago, no one associated specific activities or practices with the word *outplacement*. Gerald Bush, author of one of the papers presented at the workshop, noted that commercial outplacement activities were not reported in U.S. industry before the early 1960s, and that the first outplacement companies were not established until the second half of the 1960s. Despite its recent origins, the field of outplacement has generated considerable commerce, interest, and expertise over the last decade. The experts gathered for this workshop discussed a wide variety of outplacement issues and practices, keeping in mind the question, "What best practices can be identified to guide organizations (specifically, the Department of Defense) in effectively managing outplacement?"

For the purpose of these proceedings, outplacement is distinguished from reengineering, downsizing, layoffs, and the like. It is defined as the processes and practices needed to manage the involuntary movement of employees out of their jobs and the organization. This focus on involuntary moves distinguishes outplacement from internal moves to other jobs in the organization and from voluntary moves out of the organization. Downsizing or reengineering are terms that can be used to encompass all such moves.

The workshop focus on outplacement is a narrow one within the context of ideas and practices used to restructure organizations and develop jobs. For example, employees can be retrained and redeployed within an organization; joint community, government, and organizational efforts can be combined to develop closing facilities as business incubators for jobs; reorganization may be done to prevent the need for outplacement altogether. The Department of Defense is aware of the breadth of reengineering and downsizing alternatives that can be used in addition to involuntary outplacement, and it has considered and implemented many of them since 1989. Despite ongoing efforts to locate and develop internal employment for its civilian workforce, the Department of Defense still faces the need to outplace. The goal of the one-day workshop was to bring together some of the best people and ideas from research and practice in a lively discussion with representatives of the Department of Defense.

WORKSHOP MODEL OF OUTPLACEMENT

The workshop focus was clearly on the results that organizations want from investments in outplacement and the activities and practices most likely to achieve them. It is clear from the papers and presentations that organizations cannot manage outplacement without understanding the community in which downsizing and outplacement will occur and the individuals that outplacement will affect. Furthermore, there is no single best way to do outplacement. Each organization must take stock of its own situation and identify the types and the mix of outplacement practices needed.

Figure 1 presents a model of outplacement as it evolved from the workshop papers and presentations. The figure lists differences in the results, practices, and major considerations faced by organizations, communities, and individuals involved in outplacement. These workshop proceedings are based on this model.

Organizational Focus

The focus of the workshop was on organizational concerns in outplacement. Although organizations may differ in their priorities, most want some combination of the results shown in Figure 1. Organizations want to manage outplacement so that their reputations as a good employer, a good place to work, and an employer of choice are maintained. Most want to minimize potential litigation, as well as control other costs associated with downsizing and outplacement practices. And most want to maintain a workforce able and willing to continue performing necessary work, either indefinitely or during the phased downsizing typical of facility, base, and plant closures.

Certain outplacement practices are common to organizations concerned with effective management:

- *Planning for downsizing and outplacement* in ways that not only meet the organization's strategic needs but also provide a solid and unbiased foundation for answering questions about who remains and who goes;
- *Communicating* in ways that cover a spectrum from the initial downsizing announcement to the training of supervisors in the content and form of exit interviews;
- *Providing resources for the transition* of employees out of the organization, ranging from retirement options, to extended leaves of absence or other training opportunities, to fully equipped off-site career centers staffed to assist employees in dealing with job loss and finding a new job;
- *Customizing transition programs* to meet the specific needs of the organization and to accommodate workforce diversity; and
- *Monitoring all aspects of the transition*: the numbers of employees using different transition options, the rate and quality of reemployment associated with career centers, the morale of the remaining or "surviving" workforce, and so forth. The results of monitoring inform the organization's future decisions about the investment of resources and customization for outplacement programs.

	Outplacement Practices	Desired Results	Major Influences
COMMUNITY	Developing jobs Coordinating community resources Monitoring	Effective social service Economic vitality **New employment contract**	Availability and centralization of services Size/diversity of businesses and labor force Level of unemployment
ORGANIZATION	Planning Communicating Resource transition center Monitoring Customizing	Maintain reputation Minimize litigation Control costs Maintain workforce capabilities **New employment contract**	Size/centralization/locations Extent of downsizing (timing and head count) Workforce demographics Business mission
INDIVIDUAL	Grieving Assessing/planning Building support Marketing skills Searching for jobs Training	Reemployment: speed quality earnings Minimize stress/disruption **New employment contract**	Resilience/self-esteem Family support/finances Occupations/skills Age/gender/ethnicity

FIGURE 1 Workshop Model of Outplacement

However, organizations differ along many dimensions that influence their choices about outplacement practices. For example, differences in organizational size (and resources), differences in the centralization of management decision makers, and the geographic location of major facilities will all affect organizational planning and customization of outplacement practices. The organization's business mission, the extent of downsizing anticipated, and the nature of the organization's current workforce and the workforce to be downsized (in terms of numbers, skills, tenure, age, gender, and so forth) will also influence outplacement choices.

For example, consider two hypothetical organizations: Weber, Inc., and Burns & Stalker Associates. Weber, Inc., is a *Fortune* 1,000 firm, employing over 25,000 people, and its facilities, including headquarters, are centralized in the Atlanta metropolitan area. Weber is in the process of downsizing about 10 percent of its workforce, mostly professional and managerial employees with 10 to 15 years tenure. The downsizing complements other company efforts to reduce management hierarchies and streamline decision making in a highly competitive and unpredictable business environment. The downsizing is a first for Weber and is scheduled to occur over the next three years.

In contrast, Burns & Stalker Associates is a much smaller firm, employing only about 5,000 people in facilities scattered across the United States, mostly in rural labor markets. Burns & Stalker Associates plans to completely close one of its facilities, letting go 750 employees over the next year. These employees are, on average, young (under 35), with company tenure of under 10 years. They have manufacturing assembly and craft skills. The Burns & Stalker facility has been operating in this small rural community for generations, and, although there have been frequent layoffs and recalls, no one ever thought closure a real possibility.

These two organizations are both planning, communicating, resourcing the employment transition, and customizing and monitoring the process, but with differences. Weber, Inc., is planning downsizing with an eye to future peaks and valleys in its demand for labor. In addition to retirement options, Weber, Inc., has planned a series of workforce "buffers" that will help maintain some contact with employees (short of keeping them on the full-time payroll) in anticipation of future periods of high labor demand. Examples of buffers include extended leaves of absence and job banks in which selected employees can enroll for contract jobs within the company.

Company communications with employees highlight this notion of a flexible workforce, spelling out which employees will be eligible for buffering options and which will be permanently outplaced. As part of the communications process, supervisors are being trained to conduct outplacement interviews and are given information on benefits, severance, references, and last day of employment for each employee.

In addition to buffers such as retirement, leaves, and contract jobs, Weber, Inc., has provided resources for an off-site career center in the Atlanta area. This career center is customized to serve outplaced professionals and managers. Its expert staff offers one-stop emotional and financial counseling, career guidance, and training for job search skills. The center offers work space, phones, computers, Internet access, and job postings. Finally, Weber, Inc., has developed baseline measures to monitor costs, use, satisfaction levels, and the like for its buffers, including its career center.

Outplacement planning at Burns & Stalker Associates has been allocated to management at the facility to be closed. The planning focuses on the order in which employees will be outplaced and when their outplacement will occur as operations wind down. The company needs to maintain some personnel until closure. Communications include an initial company-wide announcement of the closing, followed by meetings with groups of employees. Letters are being sent to individual employees and their families; these letters detail benefits, severance, and other relevant news about the outplacement process and individual employees' rights. Press releases are being provided to local media. Supervisors are receiving short training sessions on how to handle outplacement interviews. A counselor is available to assist with these interviews.

Burns & Stalker has involved the community in its planning process via a community-wide task force. Task force members include: local and state unemployment workers, social service workers (alcoholism, psychological counseling, clinical social workers, welfare representatives, etc.), bank representatives and financial/tax counselors, people from the surrounding training institutions, other local employers, career counselors, and police and hospital workers. This task force is helping to centralize and coordinate services to assist employees in dealing with job loss, assessing skills, and searching for new jobs. Burns & Stalker has rented space at a local community college to be used as a career center during working hours several days each week. Local service representatives spend regular hours at the center each week and set up appointments for different types of counseling and career guidance. The people from the local branch of the state unemployment service and instructors at the community college provide job search workshops, including sessions on resume writing, interviewing, and networking. Finally, Burns & Stalker is monitoring how many employees retire, relocate, get jobs in the area, delay reemployment to get additional training, and become self-employed.

Individuals and Communities

Organizations cannot effectively manage outplacement without understanding and accommodating the individuals and communities involved. Figure 1 suggests that the outplacement results that individuals and communities desire differ from those that organizations desire. Most individuals want to be reemployed as quickly as possible, ideally in jobs that match their skills and offer earnings similar to those of their former jobs. They want to minimize the stress and disruption associated with job loss, job search, and adjustments to new jobs for both themselves and their families and friends. Communities want to minimize the stress outplacement imposes on social services, police, and local businesses while continuing to provide all services as effectively as possible. Most communities also want to cooperate with organizations in helping individuals find reemployment in order to maintain the economic vitality of their area.

Like organizations, both individuals and communities differ in terms of the major considerations that influence their choices about the outplacement practices that are best for them. Weber, Inc., has tried to accommodate the community and the individuals who will be losing their jobs in its outplacement practices. For example, its facilities are concentrated in the major metropolitan area of Atlanta. The company has hired experts to staff its career centers, and they are expected to coordinate with the many social and other services the community provides for outplaced employees. Some dollars have been allocated to the local social services to offset the anticipated increase in demand. Weber, Inc., has hired recruitment experts to help identify and develop area job opportunities for professionals and managers, and Weber's top managers have also talked to their contemporaries in other organizations about job opportunities. The consultants hired to run Weber's transition center have proprietary job banks that consist of electronic databases listing national, regional, and local employers seeking specific types of skills and experience. Transition center participants from Weber assess their own skills and experience and match these with jobs found in the database. Finally, Weber, Inc., has tailored the assistance at its career centers to meet the needs of the professional and managerial employees who have been with the organization for most of their careers. The counseling for grieving and for assessing skills and planning for a new job, as well as the workshops for marketing skills and building networks, are all geared to these particular employees.

Burns & Stalker has also recognized community and individual needs in its outplacement efforts. The company has directly involved all the community in these efforts. The company/community task force is the touchstone for job development and community services. Although the company has directed some dollars to the task force to offset increased demand for community services, the task force has also been charged with using all potential public sources of funding. The labor market surrounding the closing Burns & Stalker plant is small and heavily dominated by manufacturing. As a result, the company/community task force has become actively involved in job development, including opportunities for self-employment. The company/community task force has conducted surveys of displaced worker skills and of job opportunities at regional employers and set up job fairs to help match workers with opportunities. Finally, the counseling, planning, and training offered to outplaced employees has been tailored to relatively young manufacturing and craft workers. Counselors understand that, for many of these people, Burns & Stalker has been like a part of the family for at least two generations.

The model of outplacement in Figure 1 and the two hypothetical companies described serve to illustrate that organizational outplacement practices can be viewed as a continuum of choices: from no planning to extensive planning (as in the case of Weber, Inc.), from no communications to extensive communications, from no customizing to highly specialized programs, and so forth. An organization's choices about outplacement practices will be influenced by considerations such as its size, the extent of the downsizing, its business mission, and workforce demographics. In addition, the organization must understand the needs of the employees being outplaced and the community that will be serving their needs in order to manage outplacement effectively. In short, although there may be generic "best practices" in outplacement, the development, mix, and emphasis among practices is unique to each organization and the individuals and communities involved.

The New Employment Contract

There was particular discussion at the workshop of one outplacement result: the new employment contract. The fundamental difference between the new employment contract and the one that has been characteristic of many organizations is that, under the new contract, the organization makes no promises about a long-term career. The key phrase used at the workshop and often heard in organizations today is, "we offer employability, not employment." That is, organizations now offer individuals paid opportunities to develop skills. These skills will be employed by the organization contingent on its demand for them, or individuals can use these skills to pursue other opportunities in the job market, including self-employment and contracting.

The new employment contract has outplacement implications for organizations, communities, and individuals. For organizations, the new employment contract implies that downsizing may be a stable feature of internal labor markets, so employees' job search skills should be kept current whether they are directly in line for outplacement or not. In its planning, communications, and training, the organization needs to recognize the new contract so that both continuing employees and short-term and contract employees understand and are prepared for it. Moreover, if organizations are to be involved in outplacement as an ongoing activity, then more systematic evaluation of outplacement practices is needed to determine what works and what doesn't. For individuals, the new employment contract requires a mental framework encompassing ongoing development of skills, marketing of skills, more flexibility about work arrangements and environments, and continued networking to keep in touch with work opportunities. Finally, for communities, the new employment contract means that the demands made on social, training, and financial services by outplacement will become a more permanent feature of community life. Communities need to start planning, coordinating, and funding services to meet such ongoing demands.

PLAN OF THE PROCEEDINGS

The workshop model of outplacement presented above is used throughout the rest of these proceedings as an organizing principle. Part I begins with a commentary on two of the three papers commissioned for the workshop. These papers are included in Part I, and summarize the psychological and labor market research on outplacement. Part I ends with a summary of remarks by Amiram Vinokur, a social psychologist whose research examines programs to assist people in job search.

Part II includes a brief overview, a paper by Gerald Bush summarizing organizational outplacement experiences, and the remarks of five industry participants whose organizations have ongoing outplacement programs or who are actively engaged in outplacement as consultants.

Part III concludes the proceedings with a closer look at the civilian outplacement task facing the Department of Defense. The implications of the workshop model, the papers, and participants' remarks that are especially relevant for the Department of Defense are highlighted.

PART I

Outplacement Research and Expertise

Two papers prepared for the workshop provide an overview of the psychological research related to the effects that outplacement practices can have on employees and on reemployment, as well as the research on the effectiveness of labor market programs designed to achieve reemployment. Paper authors include: Connie Wanberg of Kansas State University and Leaetta Hough of the Dunnette Group; and Duane Leigh of Washington State University. Amiram Vinokur, a social psychologist and research scientist at the Institute for Social Research at the University of Michigan, presented the results of his research on the JOBS Project.

OVERVIEW

In "Unemployment and Outplacement: Evidence and Insights from an Organizational Psychology Perspective," Connie R. Wanberg and Leaetta M. Hough present evidence that outplacement and unemployment are stressful life events that can have a negative impact on individual and family health. They note that individuals vary in their abilities to cope with job loss, although there is evidence that the way an organization handles outplacement can mitigate individuals' negative emotions. Wanberg and Hough add that this applies to individual employees who are staying with an organization (survivors), as well as those who are leaving. As the workshop model suggests, a desired outplacement result for individuals is the effective management of stress, and it appears that the way the organization manages outplacement practices can help achieve this result. The authors also draw distinctions between outplacement practices undertaken by the organization as part of the management process (planning, communicating, resourcing the transition, etc.) and those undertaken for departing individuals in finding jobs (emotional counseling, career assessing and planning, training, etc.). They review some empirical studies of outplacement practices, emphasizing that such evaluation is scarce. Also hard to find is information on how to evaluate the effectiveness of outplacement services offered by particular consultants. Finally, Wanberg and Hough review evidence on how the effectiveness of outplacement practices may vary with individual demographic differences (age, gender, race, etc.) and individual social psychological differences (self-esteem, limited support networks, scarce financial resources). The implication is that outplacement practices may require some customization in order to have the desired results for different groups or individuals.

The second paper, "Reemployment: Labor Market Barriers and Solutions," by Duane E. Leigh provides an overview of publicly funded labor market programs designed to assist outplaced (or displaced) workers in getting reemployed as quickly as possible in jobs that offer earnings potential similar to the jobs lost. He summarizes these programs in four categories: programs to speed up reemployment, programs to replenish earnings, programs to replenish human capital (training), and programs for self-employment. Leigh reviews considerable evidence showing that job search assistance programs designed to speed up reemployment are effective and relatively low in cost. These programs encompass many of the resources typical in organizational career transition centers: career testing and guidance, workshops on job search skills, centers for job posting and advertisements, and some counseling. Job search assistance programs appear to be especially effective in speeding up reemployment if they are used shortly after a worker becomes unemployed. Leigh reviews the mixed evidence on the effectiveness of a number of other programs for reemployment, income replenishment, and training. He notes common problems in drawing conclusions about these programs. One is that unemployed people do not use the programs frequently enough, as is the case for relocation and self-employment programs. Another is that they do not use intervention programs early enough, often waiting until their unemployment or severance benefits run out before beginning job searches. A third problem is that employers do not use the programs frequently enough, as is the case for assisted on-the-job training programs. These are problems all organizations are likely to face in their efforts to outplace employees. Leigh's summary suggests that organizations should definitely fund transition centers and job search assistance for departing employees and concentrate on getting employees to use these services as soon as their outplacement status is known. Finally, Leigh reminds organizations of the public resources that can be found in their communities.

Part I ends with a summary of Amiram Vinokur's presentation on the JOBS Workshop and Project at the Institute for Social Research, University of Michigan. This workshop has been very successful in assisting recently unemployed people to find new, high-quality jobs and in energizing and motivating people to continue looking for work in the face of many setbacks. The importance of job search assistance has been echoed in all the papers, and the experimental evidence presented by Vinokur reinforces its importance. Vinokur outlines some of the unique features of the JOBS Workshop that its creators believe to be responsible for its success.

UNEMPLOYMENT AND OUTPLACEMENT: AN ORGANIZATIONAL PSYCHOLOGY PERSPECTIVE

Connie R. Wanberg, Kansas State University, and
Leaetta M. Hough, The Dunnette Group, Ltd.

Unemployment rates have been on the decline in the United States, and the number of layoffs has appeared to be on the decline as well. Then, in January 1996 AT&T announced that it was laying off 40,000 employees with 70 percent of the layoffs scheduled during the coming year (Sloan, 1996). AT&T is not alone in its intention. Apple Computer expects to lay off between 500 and 2,000 of its 13,000 employees in the next year (*Manhattan Mercury*, 1995). The Department of Defense is also in the midst of laying off thousands of military and civilian employees (Ricks, 1994). Indeed, the Army has reduced its active-duty force from approximately 710,000 to 540,000 and expects to cut an additional 45,000 positions over the next three years (Harvey, 1995). Restructuring, with its apparently inevitable downsizing, continues at a rapid pace as organizations in both the public and private sectors struggle to respond to rapidly changing political and economic conditions. In fact, the downsizing phenomenon has become so pervasive that we may not always associate it with unemployment. Unfortunately, we thereby underestimate the overall impact of downsizing.

The impact of losing one's job and the resulting unemployment is enormous. For most, it represents a crisis. Although no two persons experience such loss in exactly the same way, if it occurs, it is likely one of the most significant events in an individual's life. In this paper, we review the psychological impact of unemployment for the individual, the trend in this country for organizations to utilize outplacement consultants, and the content and relative effectiveness of outplacement services.

The Psychological Impact of Unemployment

There has been a great deal of research in the psychological literature focused on the impact of unemployment. These studies, going back to the Great Depression, have shown that unemployment tends to be a stressful life event, having an impact on individuals' psychological and physical health and on family relationships. It is common for individuals to experience feelings of anxiety, depression, shock, uncertainty about the future, anger, bitterness, resentment, shame, and loss of self-respect following job loss (e.g., Eales, 1989; Fineman, 1983; Hepworth, 1980; Swinburne, 1981). Individuals may suffer from increased physical symptoms because of the strain of job loss or because of financial deprivation and resulting poorer nutrition, housing, clothing, and heating (Kessler et al., 1987; Warr and Jackson, 1984). O'Brien and Kabanoff (1979) reported that unemployed participants in their study experienced a higher number of physical symptoms including allergies, bronchitis, coughs, colds, and shortness of breath, than an employed comparison group.

Despite the fact that unemployment tends to be a stressful life event, there are wide individual differences in the ability to cope with job loss. Recent research has investigated what factors influence individuals' reactions to unemployment. Financial hardship (having difficulty making ends meet) and high employment commitment (meaning work is very important to the individual) have been associated with lower well-being during unemployment (see Jackson et al., 1983; Turner et al., 1991). Social support, high self-esteem, perceived control over the situation, and high time structure (the ability to keep busy and productive during unemployment) have been associated with higher well-being during unemployment (see Feather and Bond, 1983; Latack et al., 1995; Turner et al., 1991). The procedures used to manage a layoff may also affect emotional reactions to job loss. In a sample of recently laid-off individuals, Bunce et al. (1996) found low levels of mental health among those who (1) felt there had been bias in the layoff decision-making process, (2) had not been given an adequate explanation about why the layoff was occurring, and (3) were not given the opportunity to appeal their termination. In contrast, individuals who felt their organization tried to be fair and just during the layoff process experienced higher levels of well-being following job loss.

While a great deal of research has focused on the impact of unemployment for individuals who have lost their jobs, fewer studies have assessed how organizational layoffs may impact individuals who are retained by the organization (layoff survivors). A recent series of studies has shown that organizational layoffs may have a substantial impact on layoff survivors (see Brockner, 1988). Productivity and job satisfaction may decrease among survivors, due to excessive workloads, feelings of guilt over the layoffs of coworkers, fear of future layoffs, and reduced commitment to the organization. For example, a study conducted at West Point found a trend for officers not laid off in the military's current downsizing efforts to show reduced commitment to the service (Ricks, 1994). Organizations that hope to reduce the impact of layoffs on both victims and survivors should strive to make unbiased, ethical, and accurate layoff decisions, communicate information about the layoff and layoff decisions clearly and respectfully, give employees advance notice of the layoff, provide opportunities to correct errors, and provide adequate severance or outplacement benefits (see Konovsky and Brockner, 1993).

In recent years, outplacement firms have begun to play an increasingly large role in helping organizations to effectively plan and conduct their downsizing efforts and in assisting laid-off individuals in securing employment. According to Pickman (1994), there are at least 300 outplacement firms in the United States, and revenues within these firms have increased dramatically in the past decade. A recent survey by the Association of Outplacement Consulting Firms International showed that 96 percent of *Fortune* 1,000 companies use outplacement firms (Mike Corbin, personal communication, November 11, 1995). Whereas in the past outplacement services were provided solely to senior executives, outplacement today is a service appropriate for individuals at all organizational levels (Sweet, 1989). The remainder of this paper discusses outplacement practices, the effectiveness of outplacement efforts, recommendations for choosing a reputable outplacement firm, the role of individual differences in the provision of outplacement services, and future research needs relevant to the provision of outplacement services.

Outplacement Programs and Practices

Outplacement is both an *organizational* process and an *individual* process. From an organizational perspective, outplacement includes (a) identifying individuals whose employment is to be terminated, (b) training the people who inform employees of their termination, (c) informing employees of their termination and their severance/benefits package, (d) counseling survivors to reduce the negative effect on morale, (e) communicating a message to the community designed to preserve the company's image, and (f) planning the strategy, policies, procedures, timing, and logistics of the entire organizational process.

From the perspective of the individual whose employment is being terminated, needed outplacement services include (a) emotional and social support to cope with the situation and to stay motivated and committed to the job search, (b) information and advice on making financial decisions and adjustments, (c) guidance with examining and developing career goals, (d) information, advice, training, and feedback on planning and conducting a job campaign, and (e) administrative support.

Outplacement consultants typically refer to the organization as the client because it is the organization that pays for both the organizational and individual outplacement services. However, the organization and individual whose employment is terminated have different and sometimes conflicting needs.

Services Available to the Organization

Outplacement consultants provide a variety of services for contracting organizations. The client organization determines the comprehensiveness of services desired.

Planning the Process The strategies, policies, procedures, and timing of outplacement activities and events are very important. Considerable planning and coordination are required. One decision is, of course, whether or not to have outside consultants or internal staff provide the organizational and individual outplacement services. Consultants are sometimes brought in early enough to help the organization plan the entire outplacement process.

Deselection Decisions The organization must decide on the criteria and processes it intends to use to identify individuals whose employment is to be terminated. The organization needs to decide how many and who to terminate and for what reason. (If an employee is terminated for cause, i.e., termination is performance-based, different procedures are typically needed.) The organization should think strategically about the skills and abilities needed in its workforce to compete in the future. The strategies used to decide who and how many people to terminate should be procedurally fair, perceived as fair, and legally defensible. Some outplacement consultants provide advice on performance appraisal procedures and strategic planning that may help the organization develop and implement fair and defensible outplacement strategies and policies.

Training the Person Who Conducts the Termination Interview The person assigned to conduct a termination interview should receive training. Such an assignment is very difficult and uncomfortable. It can be done poorly and thereby increase the trauma for the person whose employment is being terminated as well as increase the probability of lawsuits and negative reactions from other employees and the community when word spreads about how it was "mishandled." Many outplacement consultants provide training and advice on how to conduct the termination interview.

Conducting the Termination Interview The employee needs to be informed of his or her termination, the reasons for it, and his or her severance package and benefits. Ideally, the person will also have the opportunity to meet immediately with an outplacement counselor to begin the process of adjusting to the new life circumstances and finding new employment.

Counseling Survivors Those persons who are not terminated need to be informed of what has or is about to occur. If outplacement services are provided to persons who are terminated, part of the communication can focus on the quality of the treatment the individuals are receiving. The social conscience of the organization can be legitimately emphasized. The organization also needs to develop a strategy for helping the survivors adjust to the situation. Part of the adjustment may involve performing other or more work, duties that were previously performed by the persons who were terminated. Survivors may also need to adjust to what is perhaps a new reality—the employment contract is no longer a guarantee of job security. Some outplacement consultants provide advice on what and how to communicate with the remaining staff, some provide advice on how to restructure and reassign work to the remaining staff, and some provide counseling for those survivors that remain with the company.

Communicating with the Community An organization is typically concerned about its public image and correctly perceives a layoff, especially one that will affect the community, as having a likely negative effect. The outplacement consultant may provide advice about procedures that aid the community in responding to the situation as well as help draft the message that is released to the public.

Services Available to the Individual

Outplacement consultants provide a variety of services for the individual whose employment has been or is being terminated. The services may be provided to the individual in a one-on-one or group setting. Again, the client organization typically determines the comprehensiveness and type of service provided to individuals who are being laid off. The level of services usually depends on the organization's budget, as well as the employee's organizational level, length of service, and reason for termination (Davenport, 1984).

Emotional and Social Support Reactions to involuntary job loss have been likened to the grieving process. Schlossberg and Leibowitz (1980) identified five stages: disbelief, sense of betrayal, confusion, anger, and resolution. Other people have identified other, but similar, stages. Whatever labels are attached, the individual needs to cope with the depression, anxiety, and loss of self-esteem that are well-documented reactions to losing one's job. Outplacement counselors typically provide emotional support important to an individual struggling to cope with his or her emotions. Outplacement consultants advise the contracting organizations that, the sooner this process begins, the more quickly the activities that focus on reemployment can begin. Indeed, outplacement consultants are sometimes available as soon as employees have been informed of their termination.

Empirical support has been shown for the need for outplacement services to help individuals resolve some of their feelings about job loss. Spera et al. (1994), for example, found that unemployed professionals who were asked to write about their thoughts and emotions regarding their job loss for 20 minutes a day for 5 consecutive days were reemployed faster than two comparison groups. Spera et al. noted that the writing generated by the professionals was full of anger and hostility. They suggest that perhaps the writing helped the individuals work through their negative feelings, and that perhaps it helped the individuals to present a more positive outlook during job interviews.

One's job or work is for many people an important element in shaping their identity, self-worth, and status. Thus, one of the difficult events an individual encounters is informing friends and family. Many outplacement consultants help the individual through this stage and even provide counseling services to spouses and significant others. Once family and friends are informed and are coping with the news, they can become important contributors to a positive employment outcome. Social support has been shown to be a very important factor in the individual's self-esteem and motivation to seek and persist in seeking employment (Caplan et al., 1989; Kahn and Antonucci, 1981; Vinokur and Caplan, 1987; Wanberg et al., in press). As Caplan et al. (1989) demonstrated, consultants, peers, friends, and spouses can provide social support that is critical to the employment outcome.

Another variable that impacts mental health is the ability to keep busy and structure one's time. Hepworth (1980), Feather and Bond (1983), Kilpatrick and Trew (1985), and Wanberg et al. (1996) have all shown that activity and structured and purposeful use of time are positively associated with mental health. The outplacement consultant has an important role in encouraging and supporting the individual in structuring his or her time effectively.

Financial Decisions and Adjustments The individual often has a number of financial decisions to make regarding his or her severance package and benefits. Outplacement consultants often provide information about the implications of different choices or provide access to others who can provide similar advice. The individual also needs to consider the future financial impact of his or her unemployment. This typically involves changing one's lifestyle to one that requires less income, at least temporarily. Outplacement consultants often provide advice on how to assess the impact and kinds of adjustments that may be required.

Career Planning Outplacement consultants provide important assistance in working through the many career planning issues that arise following job loss. An outplacement consultant can help individuals examine their strengths and weaknesses, learn about different jobs and careers, and match their needs, skills, and abilities with the characteristics and requirements of different jobs and careers. The outplacement consultant may provide the individual with (a) questions to think about and answer (when the service is individualized, this is typically an interview), (b) tests and inventories that measure interests, needs, personality characteristics, skills, and abilities, (c) detailed descriptions and profiles of jobs and careers that include information about required skills and abilities and satisfied interests and needs, (d) directories of companies, and (e) data banks of vocational and job information. Ideally, outplacement consultants are trained professionals in providing vocational and career guidance. If effective, the outplacement experience can be an opportunity for an intense, positive self-examination of life goals and how such goals can be realized.

Planning and Conducting a Job Campaign Once the target job or career is identified, the individual must develop a job campaign plan designed to obtain job leads, market oneself, and negotiate employment offers. Each one of these involves significant effort on the part of the individual. Setbacks and rejections are difficult and can be demotivating. The outplacement consultant provides support and inoculation to help the individual remain focused and motivated even when encountering rejection (Caplan et al., 1989). In addition, the consultant provides training and information needed to plan a job campaign, market oneself, obtain job leads, and negotiate offers effectively.

Planning the search, marketing oneself, and obtaining job leads includes preparing a resume, networking, searching databases, reading newspaper advertisements, and interviewing. A plan with completion dates is helpful for focusing the individual on constructive activities throughout this phase. One of the most basic of outplacement services is help in preparing a resume. A good resume highlights the individual's special qualifications for the job. Another important feature of outplacement services is a resource library that contains reading materials and databases or access to databases on industries, companies, and jobs. The individual utilizes these resources, along with networking, to identify job leads. The outplacement consultant provides information and training on how to network and use the resource library effectively. The majority of unemployed managers and professionals find employment through networking. Although networking is not as important for clerical and blue-collar individuals, it is still an essential skill for individuals at all levels. Outplacement consultants also provide training in effective interviewing skills, on negotiating the particulars of a job offer, and how to evaluate job offers.

Administrative Support Throughout the outplacement process, administrative support may be provided to the individual. The extent of support depends on the level of the position the individual held with the client organization. Typically, the higher the position in the organization, the more generous the administrative support provided. At a minimum, administrative support includes word processing capabilities to prepare resumes and letters. At higher levels of administrative support, phone answering service, secretarial support, personal computers, fax and copy machines, and individual office space are provided.

Summary

It seems evident that outplacement consulting has the potential to be beneficial to both organizations and individuals. The contracting organization receives professional advice on planning and communicating information about their layoffs, and unemployed individuals receive emotional support and assistance with financial, career, and job-seeking issues. Outplacement purports to reduce the impact of unemployment on the individual, speed the process of reemployment, and decrease the likelihood of lawsuits targeting the downsizing organization. Yet the critical reader may wonder to what extent outplacement services have been evaluated regarding their ability to adequately achieve such outcomes. The next section focuses on measures that can be used to assess the effectiveness of outplacement services, summarizing empirical research that has focused on this issue.

Evaluating the Effectiveness of Outplacement Programs

Empirical research assessing the effectiveness of outplacement programs and services is important and necessary, although few evaluation studies have been conducted (Leana and Ivancevich, 1987; Leana and Feldman, 1992; Kozlowski et al., 1993). Organizations that purchase outplacement services want to know to what extent they are effective and worth the money they cost. Unemployed individuals do not want to waste their time and efforts participating in services that do not benefit them.

The Institute of Social Research (ISR) at the University of Michigan has conducted perhaps the largest and one of the few studies available on the effectiveness of intervention programs for the unemployed (see Caplan et al., 1989; Vinokur et al., 1991). The study focused specifically on evaluating the effectiveness of an intervention project known as the JOBS Program. The goal of the JOBS Program was to reduce the impact of unemployment on individual mental health, to prevent motivational problems during job search, and to increase placement in high-quality positions. Although the JOBS Program was not an outplacement program per se, the fundamental goals and methods of the project were comparable to those of most outplacement programs.

The 928 participants in this study were recruited from employment compensation offices in Michigan. Individuals were randomly assigned to participate in an experimental group (which involved attending eight 3-hour JOBS Program training sessions) and a control group (which involved giving individuals a brief job-seeking pamphlet). For further details regarding participant recruitment, sample characteristics, and attrition rates, see Caplan et al. (1989). The JOBS Project sessions for the experimental group occurred over a 2-week time period. These sessions included exercises and discussions aimed at establishing trust between participants and the trainers, providing social support, teaching and practicing job-seeking skills, and preparing and learning to cope with setbacks that might be faced during the job search.

The JOBS Program was very successful. Analyses completed 1 and 4 months after the intervention demonstrated that individuals that had been in the experimental group found jobs more quickly than individuals in the control group, and the jobs that they had found were of higher quality in terms of job satisfaction and pay. Individuals in the experimental group that had not found jobs had higher levels of mental health and job-seeking motivation than the unemployed individuals in the control group (Caplan et al., 1989). A long-term follow-up of the study's participants (32 months after the intervention) showed lasting effects for the benefits of the intervention for 81 percent of the individuals. A cost-benefit analysis also demonstrated that, although the intervention cost $286 per participant, the profits to the federal government and state far exceeded these costs (e.g., due to increased taxes paid by the experimental group) (Vinokur et al., 1991). Because of the success of the JOBS Program, the four primary investigators associated with the project won the National Mental Health Association's 1990 Lela Rowland Prevention Award.

The U.S. Army recently conducted a study to assess the effectiveness of its outplacement services, provided by Resource Consultants, Inc. (RCI), a firm located in Virginia (Harvey, 1995). RCI provided individuals with a 3-day outplacement workshop. Interested persons could then meet individually with a counselor and use the Army's Job Assistance Center resume software, employer databases, and reference materials. Because careful records were kept regarding use of the center's services, it was possible to compare a random sample of the individuals who had only attended the workshop with individuals who attended the workshop and participated in the additional outplacement services. The data indicated that individuals that participated in both the workshop and the additional services were significantly more likely to be employed (89.6 versus 80.9 percent) and received higher starting salaries (almost 13 percent higher) than individuals who only attended the workshop (Harvey, 1995; Hale et al., 1994). It should be noted, however, that these results could be due to higher motivation on the part of the individuals who voluntarily used the additional services. The Army Research Institute (ARI) is currently in the midst of conducting a more detailed evaluation of the outplacement services being provided to military personnel.

There are also some exemplary case studies of large-scale layoffs that include evaluations of organizational outplacement practices and their effects on individuals. Most notable here are the Leana and Feldman (1992) studies of the layoffs after the Challenger disaster in Florida and among the steel mills of the Monongahela Valley of Pennsylvania. In these studies, several organizational outplacement practices were associated with positive outcomes, such as higher reemployment and reemployment prospects (including possible relocation), higher satisfaction with jobs found, and lower psychological stress for employees who were laid off. These practices included ample advance notice of layoffs; generous severance pay and extended medical or other benefits offered to all levels of departing employees; retraining support either directly through funding or indirectly through assistance in finding funding; and support for the development of such job search skills as resume writing, interviewing, getting job leads, career counseling, and direct job placement assistance.

Hoban (1987) notes that organizations can demonstrate that they have saved money in the long run by providing outplacement services to their employees. He cites the following figures based on a review of the literature and a survey conducted in the greater Cleveland area (p.192):

> Consider an executive earning $65,000 per year. A manager at this level would typically be eligible for severance pay and benefits for up to one year. . . . If simply terminated without outplacement assistance, this individual's firing would cost the corporation $65,000 plus the cost of a year's extended benefits. Consider the alternative: outplacement with financial bridging and benefits for the duration of the job search. The outplacement fee (using 15 percent as the average) would amount to $9,750. Based on a job search of six months, which is the mid-range of the estimate for high salaried employees, this individual would receive severance pay amounting to $32,500 plus the cost of six months of extended employee benefits. Not including the benefits cost, this amounts to $42,250 when using outplacement assistance, or an estimated savings of $22,750 over the strict termination alternative.

Many outplacement firms have relied on reports of client satisfaction to support their firm's effectiveness. Grateful clients often give small gifts or letters of appreciation to their outplacement counselors and refer others who need outplacement services to the firm. Organizations interested in hiring an outplacement firm can ask for references to contact (Lee, 1990). Organizations may also develop an evaluation form for their employees to complete while using the outplacement services. Counselors can be evaluated with regard to their effectiveness, helpfulness, and level of expertise, and the quality of training workshops and materials can be rated (Henrikson, 1982).

Overall, available evidence indicates that outplacement services and programs for the unemployed can be beneficial to both the unemployed individuals and their former employers. However, the number and variety of outplacement services has proliferated in recent years, and their effectiveness may depend on the individual firm or professional chosen (Branham, 1983; Guinn, 1988). In other words, research in general may show that outplacement helps increase reemployment and improve the morale of unemployed individuals, but there may be individual firms that are more or less effective in this regard. Although there has been little or no empirical research comparing the effectiveness of different outplacement firms and the various services they provide, a few suggestions for organizations choosing an outplacement firm are noted in the next section.

Characteristics of Effective Outplacement Services

Henrikson (1982) advises that organizations contract with outplacement firms that are experienced or well established. He further advises that references be obtained from the outplacement firm and its counselors. A representative from the contracting organization may also ask if he or she may sit in on selected portions of training programs or counseling sessions.

The diversity of expertise that is required to provide the many aspects of outplacement services make it difficult for any single consultant to be equipped to handle all aspects of outplacement. An outplacement consultant needs a background in human resources, counseling, and employment law and must be very familiar with the world of work and job-seeking methods. He or she must also have respect for other individuals, even if their values differ from his or her own (Pickman, 1994). An organizational representative should ask about the diversity of expertise available on-staff at the consulting firm.

Branham (1983) suggests that it is important to inquire about how much one-on-one assessment and counseling time is devoted to each unemployed client. He suggests that at least 25 hours be spent on client self-assessment, helping the client uncover his or her job-related strengths and weaknesses. And the assessment must be interpreted or used, not just completed as a meaningless exercise. Shah (1994), writing about his experience as an outplacement client, makes this point. When he went through outplacement, he completed a 50-page questionnaire with many pages of instructions attached, met with an outplacement counselor to elaborate on many of his answers, and then wrote a 14-page summary of his experience. Shah's experience was that, although all of this assessment was completed, little to no interpretation was rendered, and he did not feel that he learned from the process.

The cost of outplacement services is also an important issue. Fees are fixed, by-the-hour, or based on a percentage of the employee's salary (Henrikson, 1982). According to Lubin (1994), U.S. companies spent an average of $2,000 per outplaced employee 10 years ago, but now spend less than $500 today. Although this is partially due to the fact that employers are now offering outplacement services to lower-level employees, it also reflects a cost-conscious attitude on the part of organizations and price wars between outplacement firms. Sweet (1989) urges employers to look at the quality of services provided and not just their cost.

Individual Differences and Outplacement

Although some general conclusions regarding what constitutes effective outplacement practices, it is possible that individual differences may moderate the effectiveness of outplacement practices that can be developed. For example, does the effectiveness of outplacement services differ by gender, race, age, or individual personality? Are there any types or groups of individuals that need special attention? Because the workforce is becoming more diverse, it is increasingly important that outplacement counselors have the ability to be effective with many types of individuals (Pickman, 1994).

Although little empirical research has focused on the role of gender, race, and age in outplacement, a few observations can be made. In terms of gender, outplacement has typically been male-dominated—most individuals referred for outplacement *and* most outplacement counselors tend to be male (Lee, 1990). A woman in outplacement may be less likely than a man to feel that her counselor understands her career situation. According to Lee (1990), networking may be more difficult for women than for men. Despite changing times, there still exists in many fields what is known as the "good old boy network," making it easier for men to make job contacts than it is for women. Women may be more likely than men to have child care or other family issues that limit their options or ability to relocate (Lee, 1990). Leana and Feldman (1991) found that unemployed women tend to rely more on symptom-focused coping (such as seeking social support) than men, and men tend to rely more on problem-focused activities such as job-seeking. Phelps and Mason (1991) report that women tend to stay in outplacement longer than men and may be more likely than men to start over as entrepreneurs or consultants. Pickman (1994) suggests it is important for outplacement counselors to work hard to empower women, be familiar with entrepreneurial options, and consider offering special support groups for women. He notes the danger, however, of targeting women for special treatment, suggesting that this may isolate them further and add discrimination against men.

Lee (1990) mentions that nonwhite (minority) individuals in outplacement may also have different needs. Similar to the situation with women in outplacement, there are only small numbers of minority outplacement clients and counselors. Minority individuals have typically received less mentoring in their careers than whites, and a less-developed network exists to help them become reemployed. It is common for African Americans to report that, in the workplace, they feel as if they are under constant pressure to prove themselves (Pickman, 1994). Pickman (1994) suggests that outplacement counselors must have the ability to be effective with ethnic groups that have different experiences, values, beliefs, and behaviors from their own. This may prove important throughout the outplacement process. As one example, when preparing individuals for job interviews, counselors will find that some individuals have been socialized to avoid eye contact and to avoid elaborating on their personal qualifications.

Some special attention may be necessary for unemployed individuals over the age of 40. Research has shown a positive relationship between age and length of unemployment (Latack et al., 1995). Individuals who have worked at the same organization for many years may have a hard time coping with their job loss (Kirk, 1994) and, since they have not been active on the job market, they may not be familiar with current job-seeking methods. Older workers may also face age discrimination and negative stereotyping. Employers may falsely believe that older workers are expensive, inflexible, resistant to change, and less productive and motivated than younger workers (Hakim, 1993). Wanberg et al. (in press) found that self-reported frequent job-seeking behavior increased reemployment for individuals under the age of 40 but did not increase reemployment for individuals over the age of 40. One interpretation of this finding may be age discrimination, but it is also possible that the older workers were less in tune with current job-seeking methods.

Another study has suggested that the individuals that may benefit most from outplacement services are those who lack a general confidence in themselves or their abilities. Eden and Aviram (1993), in a study of 66 unemployed individuals, demonstrated that individuals with low self-efficacy (a lack of confidence in one's abilities or of being successful in a variety of situations) were the most likely to benefit from an 8-day workshop that included role-playing and other exercises aimed at increasing self-efficacy in the job search context. The workshop increased reemployment among individuals with initially low levels of self-efficacy but not among those with initially high levels of self-efficacy. Individuals with high levels of self-efficacy were more likely to become reemployed whether or not they had participated in the workshop. Individuals who are concerned about financial resources, who have little social support from friends or family, and who are especially upset about being unemployed may also be ones who will benefit the most from outplacement services (Latack and Dozier, 1986).

Finally, special attention may be necessary for workers being laid off from federal employment. Individuals in these contexts often have a hard time envisioning a life outside the military or the federal government, and employers in the private sector often do not see the relevance of military service or federal employment experience to their needs (Ricks, 1994; Philpott, 1995). Military retirees have been turned down by interviewers who have said "All you have is military experience" (Ricks, 1994:A1). Even a civilian employee working for the government may face discrimination if employers feel they do not have an understanding of the "real world of business." Networking may also be difficult for military or government employees who have been forced to relocate frequently, since they may not have developed ties or relationships with private-sector employees in the various communities they have lived in (Philpott, 1995).

Several steps can be taken to increase the link between individuals in federal positions and the private sector. Philpott (1995) recommends that military and government workers frankly assess their skills and decide if there are appropriate positions available for them in the private sector. It is often desirable for individuals to consider a wide range of careers, instead of focusing on a job or career directly parallel to the previous position held. If the market is not good for the positions an individual is qualified for, he or she may need to acquire further education or training. Alternatively, an individual could work in a series of temporary positions as a means of learning about different employers and positions, as well as a means of sharpening his or her skills.

Ancona (1995) urges military individuals to have civilian friends review their resume to make sure that it is light on military jargon and that the skills that are highlighted are important to employers in a civilian context. They should also prepare for comments from employers that may suggest that they are not flexible and ready to adapt to a less structured, profit-and-loss-based business environment (Philpott, 1995). Ricks (1994) advocates that people network with ex-military or government employees in the private sector, as a means of finding people who will understand their skills and situation.

The federal employment agencies and the military can also take proactive steps to increase their employees' placement in the private sector. The Army, for example, has tried to develop a reputation in the private sector as an employer that trains young and inexperienced people and sends them out as skilled and productive employees (Harvey, 1995). The Army invites employers to enter their Job Assistance Center database at no cost. The database lists the type of skills that over 11,000 employers are recruiting for and identifies individuals with matching profiles (Harvey, 1994). Outplacement services are also provided that help individuals through the process of transferring their skills from federal employment to the private sector.

In summary, the literature suggests that outplacement efforts often need to be tailored to meet individual differences. Outplacement counselors have to be careful that they respond to the needs of all of their clients, and outplacement firms have to hire counselors who reflect the diversity of the workforce.

Research Needs

There is a need for continued research on the topic of outplacement services. Most of the literature on outplacement is practitioner-based. Although this literature provides valuable information based on consultant experience, there is little information provided from empirical research. Guinn (1988) notes that outplacement firms are often "full of recommendations that are not based on sound scientific research" (p. 58).

Research is needed, for example, to assess the relative effectiveness of various outplacement program components. No empirical work has focused on what aspects of an outplacement program are most cost-efficient and useful, or how much time outplacement counselors should focus on concrete job-seeking skills versus career goals and emotional issues within the outplacement service. Although it is likely that the exact balance is specific to each client (Branham, 1983), research on this issue would still be useful. Outplacement organizations are typically evaluated by the terminating organization in terms of how fast they are able to produce results (e.g., help find employment) for the laid-off employees. Unfortunately, this may discourage outplacement consultants from helping clients to set career goals, decide what type of position they would like to look for, and resolve emotional issues lingering from the job loss. Instead, more focus may be put on concrete job-seeking skills and trying to get the individual reemployed as fast as possible (Davenport, 1984; Bearak, 1982).

While available data seem to indicate that outplacement services are beneficial and useful to both organizations and to unemployed individuals, more evaluation research in this area is desirable. For example, it would be beneficial to conduct further research to assess the extent to which individuals receiving outplacement services are reemployed faster, receive salary increases, and are more satisfied with the jobs they find when compared with individuals who do not receive outplacement services. An optimal study on this issue would compare one group that received outplacement program services with a control group that did not on a number of variables, such as length of time to find employment, placement in chosen career, salary increases, etc. These two groups would have to be randomly assigned, and factors such as age, level of education, gender, and years of experience would have to be taken into account. Ideally, the individuals would be from the same company and laid off at the same point in time. Such a situation is not a common occurrence, however, and is almost impossible to arrange for research purposes (Lee, 1990).

Another issue of importance is how different outplacement programs compare in terms of their effectiveness. According to Lee (1990), employers who hire outplacement firms often want to know their placement rates, that is, how many individuals who use the services become reemployed. Lee suggests that this is not a good indicator of a firm's effectiveness, because virtually 100 percent of all outplacement clients eventually become reemployed. It is possible, however, to compare outplacement firms by contrasting the length of time it takes individuals in the firms to find employment, or by assessing how the salaries in clients' new positions compare with their previous salaries.

Research should also focus on the role of individual differences in outplacement and on studying what factors predict job-seeking behavior and reemployment in a general sense (e.g., see Wanberg et al., in press). These and several other topics of research relevant to outplacement services would help to increase the ability of outplacement professionals to provide high-quality services to unemployed individuals and their respective downsizing organizations.

Conclusion

Layoffs continue to occur on a large scale in the United States. Organizations have increasingly turned to outplacement firms for advice and guidance in their downsizing efforts. Current evidence seems to indicate that outplacement firms are beneficial for both the organizations that are conducting layoffs and for the individuals experiencing the layoffs. Additional empirical research would be useful to clarify the extent of the benefits provided by outplacement services and what aspects of outplacement services are most effective.

References

Ancona, P.
1995 Advice for military people adjusting to civilian life. *The Arizona Republic* (April 17):E7.

Bearak, J.A.
1982 Termination made easier: Is outplacement really the answer? *Personnel Administrator* (April):63-71.

Branham, F.H.
1983 How to evaluate executive outplacement services. *Personnel Journal* (April):323-326.

Brockner, J.
1988 The effects of work layoffs on survivors: Research, theory, and practice. *Research in Organizational Behavior* 10:213-255.

Bunce L., C.R. Wanberg, and J.F.S. Bunch
1996 Predictors and Outcomes of Victim's Perceptions of Fairness Following Layoffs. Paper presented at the 11th Annual Society for Industrial and Organizational Psychology Conference, April 26-28, San Diego, CA.

Caplan, R.D., A.D. Vinokur, R.H. Price, and M. van Ryn
1989 Job-seeking, reemployment, and mental health: A randomized field experiment in coping with job loss. *Journal of Applied Psychology* 74:759-769.

Davenport, D.W.
1984 Outplacement counseling: Whither the counselor? *Vocational Guidance Quarterly* 32:185-191.

Eales, M.J.
1989 Shame among unemployed men. *Social Science and Medicine* 28:783-789.

Eden, D., and A. Aviram
1993 Self-efficacy training to speed reemployment: Helping people to help themselves. *Journal of Applied Psychology* 78:352-360.

Feather, N.T., and M.J. Bond
1983 Time structure and purposeful activity among employed and unemployed university graduates. *Journal of Occupational Psychology* 56:241-254.

Fineman, S.
1983 *White Collar Unemployment.* Chichester, England: Wiley.

Guinn, S.L.
1988 Outplacement: Separating the myths from the realities—what professional outplacement should include. *Organizational Development Journal* 6:58-61.

Hakim, C.
1993 *When You Lose Your Job.* San Francisco: Berrett-Koehler.

Hale, T.M., G.L. Jenkins, and S.J. Harvey
1994 An Army-unique program: Job assistance centers. *Military Review* 74:71-74.

Harvey, S.
1994 Army centralizes outplacement. *Personnel Journal* 73:115-118.

Harvey, S.J.
1995 How effective are large-scale outplacement programs? *Human Resources Professional* 8:11-15.

Henrikson, D.
1982 Outplacement: Program guidelines that ensure success. *Personnel Journal* (August):583-589.
Hepworth, S.J.
1980 Moderating factors of the psychological impact of unemployment. *Journal of Occupational Psychology* 53:139-145.
Hoban, R.
1987 The outplacement option: Everybody wins. *Personnel Administrator* (June):184-193.
Jackson, P.R., E.M. Stafford, M.H. Banks, and P.B. Warr
1983 Unemployment and psychological distress in young people: The moderating role of employment commitment. *Journal of Applied Psychology* 68:525-535.
Kahn, R.L., and T. Antonucci
1981 Convoys over the life course: Attachment, roles, and social support. Pp. 253-286 in P.B. Baltes and O. Brim, eds., *Life-Span Development and Behavior, Vol. 3.* New York: Academic Press.
Kessler, R.C., J.S. House, and J.B. Turner
1987 Unemployment and health in a community sample. *Journal of Health and Social Behavior* 28:51-59.
Kilpatrick, R., and K. Trew
1985 Life-styles and psychological well-being among unemployed men in Northern Ireland. *Journal of Occupational Psychology* 58:207-216.
Kirk, J.J.
1994 Putting outplacement in its place. Journal of Employment Counseling 31:10-18.
Konovsky, M.A., and J. Brockner
1993 Managing victim and survivor layoff reactions: A procedural justice perspective. Pp. 133-153 in R. Cropanzano, ed., *Justice in the Workplace.* Hillsdale, NJ: Lawrence Erlbaum.
Kozlowski, S.W.J., G.T. Chao, E.M. Smith, and J. Hedlund
1993 Organizational downsizing: Strategies, interventions, and research implications. Pp. 263-332 in C.L. Cooper and I.T. Robertson, eds., *International Review of Industrial and Organizational Psychology.* New York: John Wiley.
Latack, J.C., and J.B. Dozier
1986 After the ax falls: Job loss as a career transition. *Academy of Management Review* 11:375-392.
Latack, J.C., A.J. Kinicki, and G.E. Prussia
1995 An integrative process model of coping with job loss. *Academy of Management Review* 20:311-342.
Leana, C.R., and D.C. Feldman
1991 Gender differences in responses to unemployment. *Journal of Vocational Behavior* 38:65-77.
1992 *Coping with Job Loss.* New York: Lexington Books.
Leana, C.R., and J.M. Ivancevich
1987 Involuntary job loss: Institutional interventions and a research agenda. *Academy of Management Review* 12:301-312.
Lee, R.J.
1990 Outplacement counseling for the terminated manager. Pp. 489-508 in J.W. Jones, B.D. Steffy, and D.W. Bray, eds., *Applying Psychology in Business.* Lexington, MA: Lexington Books.
Lubin, J.S.
1994 The layoff industry learns that the ax can be a real grind. *Wall Street Journal* November 28:A1.

Manhattan Mercury
1995 Layoffs expected at Apple soon. *The Manhattan Mercury* December 17, F6.
O'Brien, G.E., and B. Kabanoff
1979 Comparison of unemployed and employed workers on work values, locus of control, and health variables. *Australian Psychologist* 14:143-153.
Phelps, S., and M. Mason
1991 When women lose their jobs. *Personnel Journal* (August):64-68.
Philpott, T.
1995 Take charge of your career transition. *National Business Employment Weekly*, Special Edition: 4-6.
Pickman, A.J.
1994 *The Complete Guide to Outplacement Counseling.* Hillsdale, NJ: Lawrence Erlbaum.
Ricks, T.E.
1994 New military retirees turn bitter as many can't find a good job. *Wall Street Journal,* March 30:A1.
Schlossberg, N.K., and Z. Leibowitz
1980 Organizational support systems as buffers to job loss. *Journal of Vocational Behavior* 17:204-217.
Shah, H.
1994 The outplacement firm showed me the door. *Wall Street Journal,* December 5:A14.
Sloan, A.
1996 For whom the bell tolls. *Newsweek,* January 15:44-45.
Spera, S.P., E.D. Buhrfeind, and J.W. Pennebaker
1994 Expressive writing and coping with job loss. *Academy of Management Journal* 37:722-733.
Sweet, D.H.
1989 *A Manager's Guide to Conducting Terminations.* Lexington, MA: Lexington Books.
Swinburne, P.
1981 The psychological impact of unemployment on managers and professional staff. *Journal of Occupational Psychology* 54:47-64.
Turner, J.B., R.C. Kessler, and J.S. House
1991 Factors facilitating adjustment to unemployment: Implications for intervention. *American Journal of Community Psychology* 19:521-542.
Vinokur, A., and R.D. Caplan
1987 Attitudes and social support: Determinants of job-seeking behavior and well-being among the unemployed. *Journal of Applied Social Psychology* 17:1007-1024.
Vinokur, A., M. van Ryn, E.M. Gramlich, and R.H. Price
1991 Long-term follow-up and benefit-cost analysis of the JOBS Program: A preventative intervention for the unemployed. *Journal of Applied Psychology* 76:213-219.
Wanberg, C.R., R.F. Griffiths, and M.B. Gavin
1996 Time Structure and Unemployment: A Longitudinal Investigation. Unpublished manuscript. Industrial Relations Center, University of Minnesota.
Wanberg, C.R., J.D. Watt, and D.J. Rumsey
in press Individuals without jobs: An empirical study of job-seeking behavior and reemployment. *Journal of Applied Psychology.*
Warr, P., and P. Jackson
1984 Men without jobs: Some correlates of age and length of unemployment. Journal of *Organizational Psychology* 57:77-85.

REEMPLOYMENT: LABOR MARKET BARRIERS AND SOLUTIONS

Duane E. Leigh, Washington State University

Displaced workers are typically characterized as unemployed individuals with considerable work experience who have lost their jobs because of a mass layoff or plant closing. Events occurring during the first few years of the 1990s have dramatically heightened the attention paid by policy makers and the public to the circumstances of the displaced. These events include:

- Job losses in the defense sector associated with large-scale cutbacks in the federal defense budget. Adversely affected are both federal civilian and military personnel and private-sector defense industry workers.
- Concern that the implementation of the North American Free Trade Agreement (NAFTA) would cause U.S. producers to shift operations to other countries, thereby eliminating domestic jobs.
- The perception that corporate restructuring during the 1990–1991 recession and the years immediately following is, for the first time, substantially increasing joblessness among white-collar workers outside manufacturing as well as blue-collar workers in the manufacturing sector.

Because their job losses follow from industrial restructuring or changes in public policy, displaced workers face a low probability of being recalled to their old jobs or even to similar jobs in their old industries. Thus, they face the unattractive prospect of testing the labor market with job search skills likely to be rusty from lack of use, with little current information about job opportunities outside their immediate industry, and with firm- and industry-specific skills the value of which may have to be written off as obsolete.

A large literature exists indicating that displaced workers suffer sizable earnings losses associated with lengthy periods of postlayoff joblessness and lower wages upon reemployment. A recent study by Jacobson et al., (1993a, 1993b) provides a comprehensive picture of the magnitude of these earnings losses. Using longitudinal data covering the 1980–1986 period for high-tenure workers in Pennsylvania, the authors find that earnings losses of displaced workers average about $9,000, or 40 percent of prelayoff earnings in the year following displacement. The size of these losses declines somewhat over time, since almost all displaced workers find stable employment after six quarters of unemployment. But even during the fifth year after job separation, lower-wage reemployment jobs led to earnings losses that average approximately $6,500, or 25 percent of former earnings. Moreover, earnings losses associated with temporary layoffs and wage reductions began even before workers were permanently separated from their firms. Taking into account the prelayoff earnings dip, the period of postdisplacement joblessness, and lower reemployment wages, Jacobson et al. (1993a) calculate that the present value of earnings losses for a typical displaced worker is on the order of $80,000. Earnings losses of this magnitude suggest the desirability of public policy intervention to assist the reemployment of displaced workers.[1]

It should also be emphasized that these earnings losses are not uniform. In general, the literature suggests that earnings losses are especially large for displaced workers with lengthy job tenure with their prelayoff employers, those forced to change industry or occupation to find a new job, and residents of high-unemployment areas. Neal's (1995) recent analysis of workers put out of work by establishment closings indicates that displaced workers who find new jobs in other than their predisplacement industry earn significantly lower returns to both their predisplacement experience and their tenure than similar workers reemployed in the same industry. These results suggest that senior workers accumulate skills that are not only specific to the firm but also to the industry or particular kind of work. The value of these skills is, of course, lost when experienced workers are displaced from their jobs and obliged to switch industries to find new employment.

This paper provides an overview of policies and programs currently under consideration by policy makers that are designed to assist displaced workers in overcoming labor market barriers to reemployment. It first briefly describes major types of displaced worker programs. It then examines the empirical evidence available from demonstration projects, experiments, and ongoing programs that can be used to assess the labor market effectiveness of particular policies. In the next section, the focus shifts to new reemployment initiatives currently being tested but for which empirical evidence is not yet available. The final section summarizes the findings and discusses their implications for public policy.

Major Categories of Displaced Worker Programs

Table 1 outlines major types of displaced worker programs. These program types may be broadly stratified into two categories: programs intended to speed up the job search process and programs designed to replenish firm-specific and possibly industry-specific human capital made obsolete because the displaced worker will not be recalled to his or her old job and may not be able to find a new job in the old industry. Each of these categories is considered in turn.

TABLE 1 Major Types of Displaced Worker Programs

Program Type	Description
Job search assistance	Refers to a sequence of services designed to enhance job search skills, thereby speeding up the reemployment process. These services typically include some combination of the following: outreach; orientation; assessment and testing; job search workshops, resource centers, and job clubs; follow-up counseling; and job development and placement. Early intervention with these services is often termed profiling.
Classroom training	Classroom courses designed to enhance earnings potential by providing the job skills necessary for displaced workers to qualify for vacant jobs in expanding industries. Local postsecondary education and training institutions usually serve as subcontractors providing the actual skill training courses.
Relocation assistance	Programs designed to speed up the reemployment process by encouraging displaced workers to move from depressed to expanding local labor markets. Financial assistance is provided to allow workers to travel to job interviews in geographically distant labor markets and, if successful, to relocate their families to the new location.
Reemployment bonus	Directed at the problem that the reemployment of displaced workers may be delayed, not by inadequate job search skills, but by a lack of motivation to engage in search while drawing unemployment insurance benefits or by the natural reluctance to accept a new job offering considerably lower wages and benefits than the prelayoff job.
Self-employment programs	Allows displaced workers to continue receiving unemployment insurance benefits while they acquire basic business skills and attempt to establish their own small businesses.
Wage subsidy programs	Pays a wage subsidy to employers to encourage the hiring of targeted workers. The objective of these programs is that workers receive on-the-job training that enhances their firm- and industry-specific job skills.
Earnings subsidy programs	Programs that pay the subsidy directly to eligible workers. Their two-fold objective is to (1) target assistance to those displaced workers who have suffered the greatest losses in earnings and (2) increase the incentive to return to work, even at substantially lower wages, for those who under the present unemployment insurance system have an especially strong work disincentive.

Programs to Speed Up Reemployment

Displaced workers are typically eligible for unemployment insurance benefits to help them maintain family income during their spell of unemployment. During this period, they are required to meet work search requirements imposed by the system, and they are eligible for traditional labor exchange services provided by the U.S. Employment Service. Labor exchange in this context refers to matching unemployed workers who choose to sign up with local Employment Service offices to vacant jobs voluntarily listed with them by local employers. Job search assistance services are designed to go beyond the traditional labor exchange function of public employment agencies in terms of reaching out to the unemployed, improving their job search skills, and assisting them to locate jobs that may not be listed or advertised by employers. A menu of specific job search assistance services is listed in Table 1. Relocation assistance complements these services by providing displaced workers with additional financial resources to enable them to expand the geographic scope of their job search and, if successful, to move their families to the new location.

More experimental programs also designed to speed up the reemployment process are reemployment bonus and earnings subsidy schemes. The reemployment bonus is intended to at least partially offset the incentive of unemployment insurance recipients to delay active job search until the end of their eligibility for benefits, since benefits cease once a new job has been found. To offset this work disincentive, a lump-sum cash payment is made to those claimants who become reemployed quickly. Earnings subsidy plans increase the incentive to return to work, even at lower postdisplacement wages, by paying displaced workers who find a new job a temporary subsidy, the amount of which is proportional to the gap between pre- and postdisplacement earnings.

Programs to Replenish Human Capital

Displaced workers found to be in need of replenishing their marketable skills are usually referred to either classroom training programs or, less frequently, to firm-based training programs. In the case of classroom training, an eligible worker is often assigned a slot in a curriculum already developed by an institutional training provider subcontracting to the agency administering the program. An alternative approach allowing more individual choice is to provide the client with a voucher that he or she may redeem by selecting a curriculum provided by any one of a number of approved training institutions.

Numerous studies estimating earnings functions for U.S. workers have established that firm-based training has a higher return than other forms of postschool training (see, for example, Lynch 1992). This is presumably because the training is linked more directly to skills needed in the workplace. Recognizing the importance of on-the-job training, wage subsidy programs offer employers a cash payment or tax credit for a fixed period to hire targeted workers and provide them with sufficient skill training to ensure their continued employment with the firm after the subsidy period ends.

Self-Employment Programs

Not fitting neatly under either of the above headings are self-employment programs. Like the reemployment bonus, self-employment programs are an innovative attempt to make unemployment insurance less of an income maintenance system and more of a reemployment system. However, rather than being designed to expedite reemployment, the basic idea of self-employment plans is to develop the latent entrepreneurial talent possessed by some displaced workers. In these plans, selected workers are exempted from the usual work search requirements while they receive training in basic business skills and assistance in converting a business idea into a formal business plan. Then, with limited financial assistance, they are turned loose to develop their own small businesses.

Review of the Empirical Evidence

Evidence on many of the program types summarized in Table 1 is available from limited-duration demonstration projects and experiments and other program evaluation studies. This section reviews the empirical evidence available from a series of displaced worker demonstration projects funded by the federal government, a recent evaluation of the Trade Adjustment Assistance (TAA) program, and the unemployment insurance reform experiments.

Displaced Worker Studies

During the early 1980s, rising unemployment and an increasing number of plant closures led the U.S. Department of Labor to fund a series of demonstration projects intended to test the effectiveness of alternative reemployment services in placing displaced workers in private-sector jobs. In chronological order, these projects are (1) the Downriver, Michigan, program; (2) the Buffalo program of the Dislocated Worker Demonstration Projects, carried out at six sites across the nation; (3) the Texas Worker Adjustment Demonstration (WAD) projects; and (4) the New Jersey Unemployment Insurance Reemployment Demonstration Project. The first two of these programs are limited to male displaced auto and steel workers, and their evaluation results are based on an evaluation design in which the treatment and comparison groups of laid-off workers are drawn from different plants. The Texas WAD and New Jersey studies, discussed below, offer the advantages of including a broader spectrum of displaced workers and of implementing a more reliable random-assignment evaluation design. More information on all four projects is found in Leigh (1995:Ch. 3).

The Texas WAD Program This program targeted reemployment services to eligible workers under Title III of the Job Training Partnership Act of 1982. Title III specifically directs services to displaced workers. In each of three program sites, eligible workers were randomly assigned to either of two treatment groups or to a control group. The first treatment group was offered job search assistance services only (referred to as Tier I), and members of the second treatment group were offered the same services followed, if necessary, by more expensive classroom training (the Tier I/II sequence). Bloom (1990) reports net impact estimates showing that women may have enjoyed a permanent gain from program participation measured in terms of annual earnings.[2] For men, however, although WAD participants were reemployed sooner than otherwise would have been the case, their employment opportunities ultimately were no better than those of the control group. This result for men suggests that the job search assistance component of the Tier I/II sequence is effective in speeding up reemployment, but that the classroom training component has little impact in raising marketable skills.

The Houston WAD site allows the incremental effect of Tier I/II versus Tier I services to be directly estimated for men. Despite the higher costs of Tier II services, the evidence suggests that essentially no additional gains accrued from adding classroom training to job search assistance. Bloom (1990:139) points out that this disappointing result for Tier II services does not necessarily demonstrate that supplementing job search assistance with skill training cannot be an effective service strategy. Rather, he suggests that the blue-collar orientation of Tier II training curriculums available from a local community college was not well matched to the backgrounds and interests of the mostly white-collar participants in the Houston project.

The New Jersey Unemployment Insurance Demonstration Whereas the Texas WAD project served workers eligible for Title III programs under the Job Training Partnership Act, the New Jersey demonstration project was targeted to unemployment insurance claimants with characteristics common to displaced workers, namely, claimants older than age

25 who had at least three years of tenure with their prelayoff employer and who could not provide a date at which they expected to be recalled. The project had two primary objectives. The first was to assess the feasibility of an early intervention strategy in which the unemployment insurance system is used to identify early in the claim period unemployed workers who, in the absence of intervention, are likely to face prolonged spells of unemployment and exhaust their benefits. The second objective is to measure the labor market effectiveness of three alternative reemployment strategies.

Unemployment insurance claimants who passed through a series of screens intended to identify individuals who would benefit from early intervention were randomly assigned to one of three treatment groups or to a control group. All eligible claimants assigned to the treatment groups were offered a common set of job search assistance services early in their claim period. The first of these was an orientation session, followed sequentially by testing, a job search workshop, and finally an individual counseling session. Following the counseling session, claimants in the treatment group that received job search assistance services only were free to begin their job search.

Claimants assigned to the job search assistance plus retraining treatment were offered the opportunity to enroll in a classroom training or on-the-job training program. Acceptable classroom training programs were subject to the restriction that their expected duration not exceed six months. Employers who provided on-the-job training slots to claimants received a wage subsidy of 50 percent. All participants assigned to this treatment, whether or not they chose to participate in a classroom training or on-the-job training program, were informed of the availability of relocation assistance. Consistent with the experience of earlier demonstrations, very few Treatment 2 claimants opted to take advantage of relocation assistance. Finally, claimants in the job search assistance plus reemployment bonus group were told of the specifics of the bonus program and turned loose to begin job search. The design of the New Jersey reemployment bonus treatment and available empirical evidence are discussed later in this section.

Corson et al. (1989) present net impact estimates of treatment effects for the first year following the date of filing the initial unemployment insurance claim. These estimates for the job search assistance-only and job search assistance plus retraining treatments tell much the same story as the Texas WAD results. Namely, the job search assistance-only treatment produces quarterly earnings that are significantly higher in the first and second quarters after filing than the earnings of the control group. By the fourth quarter, however, the earnings effect of job search assistance had tailed off to essentially zero. This time pattern would be expected for an intervention intended to speed up reemployment but not to enhance earnings potential.

For job search assistance plus training, there is no evidence of either a permanent increase in earnings or expedited reemployment. Skill training is clearly not expected to speed up reemployment, but the absence of a positive effect on postprogram earnings indicates that training failed to have the anticipated impact on earnings potential. As with the Texas WAD projects, there are extenuating circumstances that help to account for this disappointing result. Corson et al. (1989:14) point to two factors that lead them to conclude that their evidence should be viewed as inconclusive rather than negative. The first is that a very low percentage of claimants (15 percent) assigned to this treatment received training services. Thus, any positive effect of training for claimants who actually enrolled in a training program would be substantially diluted. Second, the 1-year observation period measured since the date of the initial unemployment insurance claim is not long enough to accurately measure postprogram effects of retraining.

The follow-up study of the New Jersey program by Anderson et al. (1991) is useful because of its longer observation period and more detailed look at the job search assistance plus training treatment, including separate net impact estimates for classroom and on-the-job training. Focusing only on claimants who actually participated in a skill training program (as opposed to a random sample of all claimants offered skill training), classroom training is seen in Table 2 to significantly reduce earnings in the initial two quarters. This result is expected since training is likely to be ongoing during these quarters. But thereafter, classroom training increases earnings by as much as $582 per quarter relative to the earnings of claimants receiving job search assistance-only. Much larger and highly significant incremental earnings effects are observed for on-the-job trainees. The authors explain that the primary reason for these very large estimates is that, by the third quarter after the claim date, on-the-job trainees were employed for almost 11 of 13 weeks in that quarter, compared with less than 7 weeks of employment for job search assistance-only claimants. It must also be noted that only 45 individuals actually received services. On-the-job training was utilized infrequently because available slots generally offered lower wages than were thought appropriate for displaced workers.

The Trade Adjustment Assistance Study

The Trade Adjustment Assistance program was created in 1962 to provide income support and, to a lesser extent, retraining to displaced workers who lost their jobs as a consequence of trade agreement conces-

TABLE 2 Estimated Incremental Effects of Classroom Training and On-the-Job Training on the Quarterly Earnings of Training Recipients in the New Jersey Unemployment Insurance Reemployment Demonstration

Quarter	Classroom training	On-the-Job Training
1	$-458**	$1,469***
2	-635***	2,347***
3	-314	2,632***
4	195	2,995***
5	384	3,174***
6	191	2,480***
7	323	2,652***
8	505***	2,681***
9	409*	2,932***
10	582**	3,005***

NOTES: Estimates shown are relative to those for claimants who received job search assistance-only services. ***, **, and * indicate significance at the 1 percent, 5 percent, and 10 percent levels, respectively.

SOURCE: Anderson, Corson, and Decker (1991:Table III.4).

sions. Legislation passed in 1974 raised the level and duration of benefits and removed the linkage between tariff reductions and job losses by making workers eligible for adjustment assistance if expanding trade alone contributed to layoffs. Trade-displaced workers could receive extended unemployment insurance benefits (called Trade Readjustment Allowances or TRAs) for up to 26 weeks beyond the usual six months, with workers enrolled in an approved training program eligible for an additional 26 weeks of benefits. Subsequent legislation implemented in 1981 and further in 1988 reined in the generosity of the program, shifting its emphasis away from income maintenance and toward skill training. The 1988 law requires participation in an approved training program unless a waiver is received. The program has historically served blue-collar workers displaced from jobs in the manufacturing sector.

In the early 1990s, the Department of Labor initiated a major study to assess the labor market impact of TRA benefits and Trade Adjustment Assistance retraining services. In contrast to the short-duration training intended to enhance existing skills offered in New Jersey, the program funds retraining aimed at developing job skills that would allow the displaced to qualify for jobs in new occupations. Much of the training supplied is long-term (longer than a year), and local community colleges and vocational training centers are the major training providers. Benefits recipients are also eligible for job placement services provided by the U.S.

Employment Service and for relocation assistance. As was the case in New Jersey, interest was slight in relocation benefits because few TRA recipients were willing to move.

Drawing cases from 10 states, the evaluation of the Trade Adjustment Assistance described in Decker and Corson (1995) is based on interviews with nearly 4,800 sample members broken down into three groups: (1) recipients of TRA income maintenance benefits; (2) trainees, nearly all of whom were receiving TRA benefits; and (3) a comparison sample of unemployment insurance exhaustees whose previous job was in manufacturing. Further disaggregation occurs for training received in 1987–1988 and 1988–1989. To measure the labor market effects of retraining, the authors point out that the more appropriate comparison group is TRA recipients because their characteristics are more similar to those of Trade Adjustment Assistance trainees than those of unemployment insurance exhaustees.

The time pattern of observed earnings differences between trainees and other TRA recipients indicates, as expected, that trainees were foregoing short-run earnings as part of their investment in skill training. However, earnings tend to rise faster for trainees, resulting in their earnings overtaking those of other TRA recipients by the eleventh quarter after the initial claim. For both the pre-1988 and post-1988 samples, Table 3 presents estimates of the impact of training among TRA recipients for the final quarter of the 12-quarter observation period. The first row of the table shows that average earnings among trainees were $228 higher than among other TRA recipients in the pre-1988 sample, and $495 higher in the post-1988 sample. Only the post-1988 difference is statistically significant. Recognizing that differences in observable traits between trainees and other TRA recipients might lead to an upward bias, the estimates appearing in the second row adjust for a variety of personal and job-related characteristics, including age, education, and prelayoff weekly wage. Now the training coefficient becomes negative and statistically significant for the pre-1988 sample, and positive but small and statistically insignificant for the post-1988 sample.

Decker and Corson (1995) also point out that, even as late as the end of the eleventh quarter, some 5–10 percent of trainees were still enrolled in a training program. The final two rows of the table show training effects estimated omitting those trainees who were still in training at some point two or more years after their initial unemployment insurance claim. The result, as would be expected, is a larger (or less negative) estimated effect of training. Nevertheless, the final row of the table indicates that skill training did not have a substantial positive effect on the earnings of trainees, at least in the first three years after the initial unemployment insurance claim. Decker and Corson (1995:773) conclude that

TABLE 3 Estimated Effects of Trade Adjustment Assistance Training on Earnings in Quarter 12, TRA Recipients Only (standard errors in parentheses)

Sample and Inclusion of Control Variables	Pre-1988 Sample	Post-1988 Sample
All TRA recipients:		
No control variables	228	495*
	(215)	(239)
Control variables included	–416*	152
	(206)	(238)
TRA recipients excluding those still in training:		
No control variables	490	777**
	(251)	(268)
Control variables included	–206	353
	(235)	(250)

NOTE: * and ** indicate statistical significance at the 5 percent and 1 percent confidence levels, respectively.

SOURCE: Decker and Corson (1995:Tables 3 and 4).

training participation should be made voluntary rather than mandatory for TRA recipients, with the training requirement replaced with a requirement to participate in a job search program.

The Unemployment Insurance Reform Experiments

Supplementing the displaced worker demonstration projects is evidence gathered from evaluations of proposed reforms of the unemployment insurance system. All three proposed reforms were designed with the dual objectives of speeding up the reemployment of unemployment insurance claimants and reducing the budgetary costs of the system. A first set of reforms focuses on enhanced services to improve claimants' job search skills and on stricter enforcement of the work search rules that determine continuing eligibility for benefits.[3] The job search assistance treatment in the New Jersey unemployment insurance demonstration is a test of this first set of reforms. Considered in more detail here are the second and third sets of reforms involving reemployment bonuses and self-employment programs.

Reemployment Bonuses Of the four random-assignment reemployment bonus experiments implemented to date, the earliest is a state-funded program in Illinois conducted between mid-1984 and mid-1985. New unemployment insurance claimants who found a job within 11 weeks of the initial claim (the qualification period) and held that job for at least 4 months (the reemployment period) were paid a cash bonus of $500. As reported by Woodbury and Spiegelman (1987), the program's take-up rate is very high (84 percent) for those eligible, and the treatment was found to reduce unemployment benefits by $158 and unemployment duration by 1.15 weeks over the benefit year. These estimates were obtained for all workers assigned to the treatment, whether or not they agreed to participate and whether or not they actually received the bonus payment. The authors also calculate that benefits were reduced by a striking $2.32 for every $1 paid out in bonuses to claimants.

The very favorable Illinois results led to Department of Labor funding for additional experiments in New Jersey, Pennsylvania, and Washington. These experiments were designed to provide evidence on how to fine-tune the reemployment bonus concept by introducing more variation in the amount and timing of bonus payments. In the New Jersey Unemployment Insurance Reemployment Demonstration, the maximum reemployment bonus was specified to be one-half of the claimant's total entitlement, defined as a lump-sum payment capturing the stream of benefit payments to be received over the remaining weeks of unemployment eligibility. The maximum bonus could be collected by accepting a job during the first two weeks after agreeing to participate in the program at the counseling interview. After these two weeks, the size of the bonus decreased by 10 percent per week, reaching zero at the end of the eleventh week after counseling. To qualify for the bonus, the claimant's new job must be full time with a new employer. The Pennsylvania and Washington experiments offered two and three levels of bonus payments, respectively, expressed as multiples of average weekly benefit amounts, combined with two levels of the qualification period. The reemployment period was about 4 months in all three post-Illinois experiments.

As described by Meyer (1995:96–112), the subsequent bonus experiments were all found to have much smaller effects than in Illinois. In particular, bonuses reduce receipt of unemployment benefits by about one-half of a week, or about 3 percent of the average duration of receipt. Estimates in this range are about the same as those obtained for job search assistance programs, but at a much higher cost due to the bonus payments. Following a flurry of excitement generated by the Illinois experiment, the less favorable results reported for the subsequent experiments dampened economists' enthusiasm for the reemployment bonus concept. Nevertheless, a reemployment bonus was included among changes in the unemployment insurance system recommended by the Clinton administration in the proposed Reemployment Act of 1994.

Self-Employment Programs In the late 1980s, the Department of Labor initiated two demonstration projects to test the effectiveness of self-employment as an alternative reemployment strategy for unemployment insurance claimants. The Washington project began in September 1989 and supplied program services through March 1991. The Massachusetts project began in May 1990 as a 3-year demonstration project. Both projects are early intervention programs providing services that include 20 hours of training in basic business skills, counseling, and financial assistance in the form of biweekly unemployment benefits. Along with these similarities, the projects differed in two important respects. First, the Massachusetts project was targeted to unemployed workers judged likely to exhaust their benefits. The Washington project did not impose this targeting restriction. Second, the Washington project provided, in addition to regular payments, a lump-sum payment equal to remaining unemployment benefits to those who completed five project milestones, defined as completing a set of four business training modules, developing an acceptable business plan, opening a business bank account, satisfying all licensing requirements, and obtaining adequate funding.

Both self-employment demonstrations were formally evaluated using a random assignment methodology. As reported by Benus et al. (1994), the most favorable of the net impact findings is that the programs sharply increased the likelihood of self-employment and accelerated its start. These estimates were obtained over follow-up periods averaging about 21 months in Washington and 19 months in Massachusetts. Other program net impact estimates for self-employment earnings, wage and salary earnings, and employment of nonparticipants tend to show smaller or no effect. Perhaps the most important finding from the demonstrations is that interest in self-employment is not strong among unemployment insurance claimants. Benus et al. (1994:ii) comment that "while many profess an interest in self-employment, relatively few choose to pursue self-employment when the opportunity arises."

Recent Reemployment Initiatives

In addition to the reemployment services tested in the demonstration projects and experiments discussed in the previous section, it is useful to briefly consider several initiatives that have recently been implemented but for which evaluation evidence is yet unavailable. These include state programs implementing a worker profiling strategy, a training voucher program in New Jersey, and a Canadian earnings subsidy program.

Worker Profiling

The New Jersey Unemployment Insurance Reemployment Demonstration provided the empirical basis for congressional action taken in 1993 to require states to establish a system for profiling new unemployment insurance claimants. The intent of profiling systems is two-fold: early identification of displaced workers who are at risk of exhausting their unemployment insurance benefits and a linking of these individuals with appropriate reemployment services in a timely fashion. The 1993 legislation also requires claimants referred to reemployment services to participate in these services as a condition of eligibility for unemployment benefits.

The Department of Labor recently initiated a major 4-year study of state profiling systems. Hawkins et al. (1995) presents interim findings from Phase I of the study focusing on implementation of profiling systems in Delaware, Florida, Kentucky, Maryland, New Jersey, and Oregon. (Phases II and III will present net impact estimates.) The Phase I evaluation is based on the following sources of information: site visits of the research team to each of the six states, information collected from profiling proposals and administrative reports, and a customer satisfaction survey of profiled and referred claimants in the six states. Drawing on this information, the profiling systems of most states were found to provide a sequence of services including a group orientation session; an assessment interview, usually provided in a one-on-one setting; and the development of a service plan. Four states, in addition, supplied claimants with a job search workshop. Finally, all of the local sites included referrals to other services, generally referrals for education and job skills training, but also for such supportive services as child care.

The survey of customer satisfaction conducted during the summer of 1995 has the objective of providing states with early feedback on claimants' satisfaction with profiling services. Keeping in mind that profiling systems are quite new, Hawkins et al. (1995:E-9–E-10) report the following findings:

- Older workers generally were more satisfied with services than younger workers, perhaps because the program helped them address the added challenge they face in finding appropriate reemployment. Overall satisfaction seemed not to be related to claimants' previous wage level or job tenure.
- Among specific services, claimants rated development of an individual service plan as one of the most helpful. Moreover, those who reported receiving assistance in developing a plan were significantly more satisfied with the program overall than other claimants.

• More important than the receipt of any particular service was the intensity of services received. Claimants who received more types of reemployment services and those who received more hours of services were substantially more satisfied with their profiling program overall.

Training Vouchers

An important provision of the Reemployment Act of 1994 would have encouraged displaced workers to enroll in longer-term education and training programs by allowing eligible workers to qualify for up to one year of income support beyond the usual six-month maximum for unemployment insurance benefits.[4] Although the act failed to achieve congressional approval, President Clinton has continued to emphasize the importance of long-term skill training. Specifically, he proposed in his 1995 State of the Union Address the elimination of essentially all adult training programs, with the money saved to be shifted to "skill grants" that eligible workers could use to pay for training programs of their choice lasting up to two years.

In 1992 the New Jersey legislature authorized the Workforce Development Partnership Program, an important component of which is a voucher-based training program targeted to displaced and economically disadvantaged workers. (The other two key components are additional unemployment benefits during training and grants to employers for customized training services.) The maximum training grant per person is $4,000, with an additional grant of up to $1,000 if the participant requires remedial education prior to training. Training services must be provided by an approved service provider, which in practice means a proprietary school or 2-year community college.

Using the unemployment insurance system, newly displaced workers are processed through a series of screens before they are admitted to the Individual Training Grant Program. The complexity of the screening process can perhaps best be visualized in the series of steps shown in Table 4 (for more detail see Benus and Grover 1995: Exhibit 1).

A key element of the training program is the development of an individualized job placement plan designed to help place participants in training-related jobs. Following the completion of training, participants are also invited to attend a postprogram job search seminar.

Descriptive statistics supplied by Benus and Grover (1995) in an initial report of the evaluation study indicate that of over 900,000 new unemployment insurance claimants during the July 1992 to October 1994 period, about 9 percent attended a Workforce Development Partnership Program orientation meeting, and about 14 percent of those oriented received an individual training grant. The demographic characteristics of

TABLE 4 Screening Process for the Individual Training Grant Program

1. *Benefits Rights Interview.* Displaced workers file for unemployment insurance and are informed about the Workforce Development Partnership Program and other training options at their benefit rights interview.

2. *Orientation.* Those claimants who indicate an interest in training are invited to attend an orientation meeting at a local Employment Service office at which a more in-depth description of training options is provided. At the end of the meeting, a questionnaire is completed by all individuals still interested in training.

3. *Career Reemployment Seminar.* Individuals who, based on their questionnaire responses, meet targeting criteria are scheduled for a half-day career reemployment seminar. A testing and assessment interview may be part of this seminar.

4. *Meeting with Counselor.* A final determination of eligibility for the program is made at this meeting.

5. *Agreement on an Employment Development Plan and a Training Contract.* For individuals judged to be eligible, the client and counselor work out an employment development plan describing the client's training and employment goals. Then a training contract is agreed to which details the type, length, cost, and dates of training.

6. *Training Begins.*

SOURCE: Adapted from Benus and Grover (1995:Exhibit 1).

claimants oriented and grant recipients are quite similar. Compared with the typical unemployment insurance claimant, however, the grant recipients are more likely to be female, to be between the ages of 30 and 49, and to possess a terminal high school diploma or equivalency certificate. Blacks are overrepresented among grant recipients, and Hispanics are underrepresented. Approximately half of all trainees planned to enroll in a short training program of six months or less, and another one-quarter planned enrollment in programs lasting more than one year. About two-thirds of all grants ranged between $3,000 and $4,000. Net impact estimates for the individual training grant program will be available in subsequent reports.

Earnings Subsidies

Motivating the earnings subsidy as a policy intervention to assist displaced workers is evidence such as that provided by Jacobson et al. (1993a, 1993b) showing that displaced workers frequently suffer very large earnings losses. Because the gap between earnings losses and current levels of public assistance is so large, the authors (1993b:160-69) suggest that alternative policy measures should be investigated, and their preference is for an earnings subsidy program.[5]

An earnings subsidy program works by paying reemployed displaced workers some fraction of the gap between their pre- and postdisplacement earnings. In this way, the greatest level of assistance flows to those suffering the greatest earnings losses. In addition, the subsidy is restricted to those who find a new job, so that displaced workers have an incentive to return to work quickly. The unemployment insurance system also targets the greatest assistance to workers who face the most difficult transition, since workers who are unemployed longer tend to have both more difficult transitions and to receive the most assistance. However, unemployment insurance has a built-in work disincentive, since assistance ends at reemployment. This work disincentive is especially strong for displaced workers who suffer large earnings losses because the benefits are based, in part, on predisplacement earnings. Thus, regular unemployment insurance benefits might be as much as 75 percent or even higher of the wages that such workers could expect to earn in their postdisplacement job.[6]

The Canadian government is currently conducting an experiment at five sites to test the effectiveness of an earnings subsidy program for displaced workers. As described by Bloom et al. (1995), the experiment is restricted to a carefully selected subset of unemployed people who must be new unemployment insurance claimants and have been employed continuously during the 3 previous years. Claimants who meet these criteria are randomly assigned to treatment and control groups. Those in the treatment group receive an explanation of the earning subsidy plan. They then receive the subsidy if they become reemployed in a full-time job with a new employer within 26 weeks of the date of the subsidy offer, and the reemployment job pays less than the predisplacement job. The subsidy offsets 75 percent of the claimant's weekly earnings loss up to a maximum of $250 per week for a period not to exceed 24 months from the time of the subsidy offer.

To consider an example offered by Bloom et al. (1995), suppose that a member of the treatment group lost a job that paid $400 per week and then found a new full-time job that paid $200 per week within six months after receiving the subsidy offer. He or she would receive a weekly subsidy of $150 (three-quarters of the earnings loss of $200), providing a total weekly compensation of $350 for working full-time. In contrast, unemployment insurance benefits for this individual would be $220 per week. A clear work incentive exists since the earnings subsidy plan provides the claimant an earnings replacement rate of 87.5 percent for up to 24 months as opposed to a replacement rate of 55 percent offered by regular unemployment insurance for up to 50 weeks.

Bloom et al. report that, as of fall 1995, the earnings subsidy program is up and running in all project sites. Approximately 5,000 claimants are to be included in both the treatment and control groups. Program net impact estimates will eventually be obtained from a follow-up survey collecting information on employment and earnings which will be administered to sample members at 15 months after they enter the study.

Summary and Policy Implications

This paper provides an overview of major policy proposals put forward to assist the reemployment of displaced workers, subject to the limitation that the proposals discussed have been or are currently being evaluated. Broadly speaking, these proposals fall into one of two categories: policies to speed up reemployment and policies to replenish lost earnings potential. Self-employment programs, which do not fit comfortably under either heading, are also considered, but the available evidence suggests that relatively few displaced workers are interested in pursuing such programs.

Expediting Reemployment

Among policies intended primarily to expedite reemployment, a great deal of evidence is available on the effectiveness of job search assistance services; and more evidence is forthcoming as net income estimates become available from state profiling programs. This evidence consistently shows that these services are effective in speeding up reemployment. Given their low cost, they are also typically found to be cost-effective. Early intervention with job search assistance is a basic level of services that should be made widely available to displaced workers.

The existing evidence is less favorable for relocation assistance and reemployment bonuses. A reluctance of displaced workers to relocate geographically is found to limit the usefulness of relocation assistance. Early evidence from a reemployment bonus program in Illinois indicated considerable promise that bonuses effectively speed up reemployment by offsetting the incentive of unemployment insurance claimants to delay serious job search until the end of their eligibility. Three subsequent experiments suggest, however, that reemployment bonus plans are no more effective than job search assistance programs, but at much higher cost.

Earnings subsidies have also received recent attention as a policy option that meets the dual objectives of encouraging an earlier return to employment and directing assistance to the displaced workers experiencing the largest earnings losses. The Canadian government is currently implementing an earnings subsidy experiment from which net impact estimates will soon be available. This experiment should help to resolve uncertainties about the labor market effectiveness and cost of earnings subsidy programs.

Replenishing Earnings Potential

Displaced workers found to be in need of skill upgrading in order to compete effectively for jobs in growing industries are usually referred to either classroom training or firm-based training programs. Since the employer shares in the costs, firm-based programs offer the advantage of providing training that will actually be utilized on the job. A large body of evidence using nonexperimental data indicates that there is a substantial labor market payoff to company-provided training. A similar result, but for a very small number of on-the-job training recipients, is also reported for the wage subsidy implemented as part of the New Jersey Unemployment Insurance Reemployment Demonstration.

The major problem with wage subsidy schemes is not that the on-the-job training they encourage is ineffective, but that it is difficult to interest employers in hiring targeted workers. For example, Bishop and Montgomery (1986) report that employer participation rates are extremely low for four targeted wage subsidy programs in operation in the United States through 1980. Rather than the carrot of a wage subsidy, other nations, namely, France and Australia, have experimented with a stick approach of requiring employers to make training expenditures equal to a percentage of their payrolls or to be subject to a payroll training tax (see Leigh, 1995). This approach has been discussed but not implemented in this country.

Results from the displaced worker demonstrations are more mixed for classroom skill training programs. Only the follow-up study of the New Jersey unemployment insurance demonstration focusing specifically on individuals who actually received classroom training services (as distinct from the random sample of all eligible individuals offered it) yields evidence of a positive effect of classroom training above that of job search assistance only. It is worth noting that the short-term, low-cost training provided in New Jersey was designed to upgrade workers' existing skills rather than to furnish training for a new occupation. In contrast, participants in the Trade Adjustment Assistance program received longer-term training intended to equip them to enter a new occupation or industry. Evaluation results for the program are positive in the sense that the longer-term investments in classroom training allowed the earnings of the trainees to reach the level of earnings of a comparison group of displaced workers, most of whom may be presumed to be industry and occupation stayers. (Displaced workers reemployed in the same occupation and industry typically experience smaller earnings losses than occupation and industry switchers.)

On the basis of this evidence, it seems prudent to conclude that classroom training should be limited to carefully selected workers who can be matched with training curricula tailored to their backgrounds and the needs of local employers. A training voucher program appears to be an appropriate policy for allowing selected individuals to exercise freedom of choice in choosing a training curriculum while effectively utilizing the nation's extensive system of postsecondary educational institutions. Evaluation results will be available in the near future for a voucher-based training program implemented in New Jersey.

Notes

1. The usual argument for publicly funded assistance is that, whereas society as a whole benefits from maintaining a dynamic, generally open domestic economy, the inevitable adjustment costs are disproportionately borne by displaced workers. Hence, some form of compensation is due the displaced because of "fairness" considerations and the necessity of preempting political intervention that would restrict trade and the introduction of new technology.

2. In principle, the labor market effectiveness of a program is measured by comparing, say, the earnings of program participants with what their earnings would have been in the absence of the program. Of course, the level of earnings that participants would have earned in the program's absence is never observed, and thus it is termed the counterfactual. There are two commonly used approaches to obtaining the counterfactual estimate needed to obtain a net impact estimate. The nonexperimental approach uses an externally selected comparison group of workers and adjusts statistically for inherent differences between the treatment and comparison groups. In the alternative experimental approach, random assignment of eligible workers to treatment and control groups means that there are no inherent differences in the observable and unobservable characteristics of the two groups.

3. Results obtained for the job search experiments are examined in detail in Meyer (1995:112–121).

4. Providing empirical support for this provision is a widely cited study by Kane and Rouse (1995) that shows that labor market returns per year of community college credits are positive and essentially the same as the returns per year of credits at 4-year colleges and universities. Community colleges are the major subcontractor to government agencies charged with implementing retraining programs.

5. Baily et al. (1993:204) also recommend the adoption of an earnings subsidy program to help cushion the heavy financial blow associated with displacement.

6. Relative to regular unemployment insurance, unemployment insurance reemployment bonus schemes also increase the incentive to return to work. However, reemployment bonuses do a less effective job in targeting assistance to workers most in need of help because bonuses are either fixed in size or contingent on the claimant's unemployment insurance entitlement, whereas earnings subsidy plans directly relate the subsidy to the size of the earnings loss.

References

Anderson, Patricia, Walter Corson, and Paul Decker
1991 The New Jersey Unemployment Insurance Reemployment Demonstration Project Follow-Up Report. Unemployment Insurance Occasional Paper 91-1, U.S. Department of Labor.

Baily, Martin N., Gary Burtless, and Robert E. Litan
1993 *Growth with Equity: Economic Policymaking for the Next Century.* Washington, DC: Brookings Institution.

Benus, Jacob M., and Neelima Grover
1995 Exploring New Alternatives to Worker Retraining. Paper prepared for the 17th Annual Research Conference of the Association for Public Policy Analysis and Management, Washington, DC (November 2-4).

Benus, Jacob M., Michelle Wood, and Neelima Grover
1994 *A Comparative Analysis of the Washington and Massachusetts UI Self Employment Demonstrations.* Cambridge, MA: Abt Associates (January).

Bishop, John H., and Mark Montgomery
1986 Evidence on firm participation in employment subsidy programs. *Industrial Relations* 25(Winter):56-64.

Bloom, Howard S.
1990 *Back to Work: Testing Reemployment Services for Displaced Workers.* Kalamazoo, MI: W.E. Upjohn Institute for Employment Research.

Bloom, Howard S., Barbara Fink, Susanna Gurr, and Wendy Bancroft
1995 The Canadian Earnings Supplement Project (ESP): Subsidizing Reemployment Instead of Subsidizing Unemployment. Paper prepared for the 17th Annual Research Conference of the Association for Public Policy Analysis and Management, Washington, DC (November 2-4).

Corson, Walter, Paul Decker, Shari Dunstan, and Stuart Kerachsky
1989 New Jersey Unemployment Insurance Reemployment Demonstration Project. Unemployment Insurance Occasional Paper 89-3, U.S. Department of Labor.

Decker, Paul T., and Walter Corson
1995 International trade and worker displacement: Evaluation of the Trade Adjustment Assistance Program. *Industrial and Labor Relations Review* 48 (July):758-774.

Hawkins, Evelyn K., Suzanne D. Kreutzer, Katherine P. Dickinson, Paul T. Decker, and Walter S. Corson
1995 *Evaluation of Worker Profiling and Reemployment Services Systems.* Menlo Park, CA: Social Policy Research Associates (September).

Jacobson, Louis S., Robert J. LaLonde, and Daniel G. Sullivan
1993a Earnings losses of displaced workers. *American Economic Review* 83(September):685-709.
1993b *The Costs of Worker Dislocation.* Kalamazoo, MI: W.E. Upjohn Institute for Employment Research.

Kane, Thomas K., and Cecilia E. Rouse
1995 Labor-market returns to two- and four-year college. *American Economic Review* 85(June):600-614.

Leigh, Duane E.
1995 *Assisting Workers Displaced by Structural Change: An International Perspective.* Kalamazoo, MI: W.E. Upjohn Institute for Employment Research.

Lynch, Lisa
1992 Private-sector training and the earnings of young workers. *American Economic Review* 82(March):299-312.

Meyer, Bruce D.
1995 Lessons from the U.S. unemployment insurance experiments. *Journal of Economic Literature* 33(March):91-131.

Neal, Derek
1995 Industry-specific human capital: Evidence from displaced workers. *Journal of Labor Economics* 13(October):653-677.

Woodbury, Stephen A., and Robert G. Spiegelman
1987 Bonuses to workers and employers to reduce unemployment: Randomized trials in Illinois. *American Economic Review* 77(September):513-530.

REMARKS ON THE JOBS WORKSHOP AND PROJECT

Amiram Vinokur
Institute for Social Research, University of Michigan

The JOBS Workshop is the focus of a project conducted at the Institute for Social Research over the last 10 years. The project is funded by the National Institute for Mental Health, and its mission is to create programs for job search assistance that prevent the deterioration of mental health among unemployed people, and all the negative consequences of poor mental health: child abuse, spousal abuse, poor physical health, and so forth. The project is directed by several research scientists, including myself, with backgrounds in social psychology and organizational psychology. We designed the JOBS Workshop as an early intervention to prevent deterioration of mental health among unemployed people by speeding up the reemployment process. The research suggests that, when people become reemployed, their mental health is restored to the same level as when they were previously employed. In addition to speedy reemployment, in this project we have also been interested in the quality of reemployment both in terms of earnings and of people liking their new job.

The JOBS Project has been run as a scientific experiment with two very large trials—one with 900 unemployed and the second with almost 2,000 unemployed people recruited from the lines at the Michigan Unemployment Service Offices. People were approached while waiting in line and were told about two programs being offered by the University of Michigan on how to seek jobs. One was described as a self-guided booklet and the other as a 2-week series of morning sessions. Those selected had been unemployed less than 4 months and employed prior to that for at least 3 years. People 2 years short of retirement or who expected to be recalled to their jobs were also screened out. The resulting samples were demographically very similar to the unemployed population in the United States.

The results of the JOBS Workshop have been dramatic. In the first 1 to 4 months after the workshop, those who participated in it had higher employment rates and higher-quality employment than those who used the self-guided booklet. The workshop participants without jobs had higher levels of self-esteem and motivation for job search than those in the self-guided group without jobs. Two years later, those who participated in the workshop were more likely to be working full time and less likely to have switched jobs. They were also likely to be earning more per month than the employed from the self-guided group. (We have found that older workshop participants have more difficulty in finding high-quality jobs quickly than do younger participants.) Cost-benefit analyses of the workshops indicate significant gains over cost for individual participants (and for state and federal governments in terms of taxes collected).

We believe there are several unique features of the JOBS Workshop that account for its success in terms of both speed and quality of reemployment. The first of these is the extensive training provided to the trainers or facilitators who run the workshop. The workshop is run by a male-female pair of trainers who have received 300 hours of training before beginning the workshop. This training is designed to help the trainers establish themselves as experts with their workshop participants. Trainers are also taught to facilitate self-disclosure both for themselves and the workshop participants. This helps to quickly establish an atmosphere. The second unique feature of the JOBS Workshop is the use of active learning. All participants learn how to do job search by actively engaging in practice job search sessions. These sessions are designed to directly demonstrate to each participant that he or she does have what it takes to get a job. We focus on getting each participant to think like an employer. During these sessions, participants are continually coached and their behaviors reinforced by the trainers and the other participants. A third unique feature is that all workshop sessions identify barriers that participants will encounter in searching for jobs and help them prepare to "inoculate themselves" against the resulting negative feelings. This feature is meant to help people maintain their motivation and energy for the job search despite setbacks.

We have developed extensive documentation of the JOBS Workshop that includes all the information used to train the trainers as well as all the materials used in the workshops. Recently, we have been approached by the government of Finland to implement this workshop for those who are currently employed but may be laid off in 6 months to 1 year. One question we want to answer is, "Will people who are not currently without a job actually use and benefit from the workshop?" We will also be implementing the workshops for people who are recently unemployed at selected sites in California.

PART

II

Industry Experience with Outplacement

The industry executives asked to participate in this workshop have all had experience with major downsizing and outplacement efforts in their respective organizations. This experience covers total shutdowns and phased reductions-in-force, taking place in small, rural labor markets as well as major metropolitan areas, for all levels of employees and all types of skills, and, in many cases, in multiple sites throughout the United States. The range of outplacement experience represented at the workshop is relevant to the outplacement still facing the Department of Defense, particularly General Electric and Lockheed Martin, which are both defense contractors with experience in the outplacement of employees with skills similar to some of those who will be outplaced by the Department of Defense. Right Associates has also had extensive experience with outplacement for the military. The participants include: Jack Ryan of General Electric Aircraft; Susan Diamond of Right Associates; Ellen Jackson of AT&T; Anne Messenger of Lockheed Martin, and Anthony Papalia of SUNY Cortland and Smith Corona. The presentations each participant made during the workshop are summarized below.

OVERVIEW

Part II begins with an overview of outplacement experience in a paper by Gerald R. Bush. "Lessons Learned from Outplacement Practice and Experience" examines outplacement from the perspective of a manager and outplacement consultant. Bush uses details and examples to flesh out the outplacement practices listed in the workshop model—planning, communicating, and providing resources for the transition (assistance with job loss and job search). He emphasizes planning that encompasses "the well-being of employees who are leaving, *and* . . . those who are staying." Bush notes the importance of communications about outplacement not only for employees, but also for the surrounding community, the organization's customers and suppliers, the media, and the employees' families. In particular, he highlights the importance of the termination or exit interview with departing employees, noting that the quality of this interview can have a significant impact on how all employees perceive the organization. Supervisors need to be trained to get the fact of job loss across to employees unequivocally, as well as deal with the employees' reactions.

Bush briefly describes individual reactions to job loss and the effects that these reactions can have on family and community. He notes that outplacement programs need to consider individual reactions and the broader social aspects of job loss in planning outplacement programs. Finally, he outlines a framework for outplacement support of the job search that includes organizational structuring of the job search process, training for technical and job search skills, education about the new employment contract and evolving work forms such as self-directed teams, and coordination and centralization of information about funding, training, and job opportunities. The Bush paper provides good background for the remarks of industry participants.

Jack Ryan of General Electric (GE) Aircraft noted that GE has developed a model for outplacement that, although used to provide guidelines throughout the company, can also be tailored to the needs of each GE business. He then described an organizational process for outplacement that includes all the practices shown in Figure 1 (see p. 4): planning, communicating, resources for transition centers, monitoring, and customizing. Ryan reported that GE Aircraft ran two transition (career) centers between 1992 and 1995, one tailored to the needs of professionals and managers, the other tailored to hourly workers. Both centers were fully resourced—that is, they were staffed by expert consultants, ran a full complement of workshops for job search, provided counseling, and had all the material resources required (workstations, telephones, job search databases and other information on job opportunities) for finding jobs. Ryan allowed that, with hindsight, GE Aircraft wishes it had done more up-front planning for outplacement, more marketing and communicating with employees about the importance of using the transition centers, and more monitoring of data on center use. He highlighted the importance of community job development in helping people to become successfully reemployed. He also noted that coordination with community providers of services for training and social welfare has been an important part of GE Aircraft's transition center services.

Susan Diamond of Right Associates offered an upbeat picture of outplacement and reemployment. She stated that virtually all employees who want to find new jobs will do so. She emphasized that outplacement should help people not only to get new jobs, but also to find jobs that match their interests. Right Associates is one of the largest outplacement consulting firms in the world, with considerable experience with the military and defense contractors, and Diamond shared some of this experience. In doing so, she provided a clear picture of what organizations should look for in selecting outplacement consultants. At the community level, Diamond emphasized the importance of expertise and technology in developing networking opportunities and job leads. She also noted that experts know when to go out into the community to find training resources (for example, for literacy instruction) that they are not best suited to provide. At the individual level, Diamond highlighted the need to have career center staff who can not only assess client problems and skills, but also help them use this information to actively prepare for and pursue jobs. Finally, at the organization level, she discussed the need for monitoring outplacement services, using measures to gauge the quality of job development, workshops, career center use, and so forth. She also pointed out the importance of finding experts who can work with the organization from the onset of downsizing to help plan outplacement, communicate with employees, and set the stage for employee acceptance of both outplacement and the new employment contract.

Ellen Jackson of AT&T described its outplacement efforts as part of a much broader planning scenario. Since 1991, AT&T has planned and implemented a host of programs designed to buffer the ups and downs in its internal labor market demands for different types of skills. Jackson noted that this planning has been done to accommodate a more competitive and unpredictable business environment, and also as a way to offer alternatives to a workforce that wants more flexibility in balancing work and lifestyle demands. She described two buffer programs in some detail: a special leave of absence program and a program called Resource Link. This latter program selects AT&T employees who have been given termination notification and keeps them in an internal pool of talent that is contracted out to AT&T customers internally. Both these programs have been very successful, and Jackson noted that employees view them as tangible evidence that AT&T cares about them.

Anne Messenger of Lockheed Martin offered workshop participants the benefits of her 11 years of outplacement experience by emphasizing some of the more intangible "musts" that she considers essential in successful outplacement. Many of these go to the heart of what it means to consider the individual in all the outplacement planning, job development, monitoring, and so forth that goes on in most major organizational downsizing. She noted, for example, that career centers must hire "intelligent, street smart, people smart staff," and that she is firm about having staff with personal experience of job loss. She also said that the career center should look good physically, because this helps both clients and staff feel better about being there. She closed by noting that she firmly believes you can teach people how to find and secure jobs, but that it is more difficult to teach them how to understand the new employment contract. The latter requires a mental shift that is hard to accomplish.

Anthony Papalia of SUNY Cortland has worked in outplacement for 20 years and was closely involved with the shutdown of Smith Corona in the small, rural community of Cortland, New York. Nearly 2,700 employees lost their jobs in that shutdown. He described the task force and the steering committee that were set up to involve company and community in outplacement efforts. He noted that a high level of community involvement was necessary to find jobs, provide training, deal with financial and health problems, and provide warning to local businesses that their own balance sheets would be affected. He detailed some of the training efforts required to bring long-term employees' skills up to standard so that they could find new jobs. On a sober note, he warned about the need for increased security measures when terminations are announced—not only at the company but also at the homes of key executives. To balance this out, he closed by saying that it is essential in all outplacement efforts to help employees who have lost their jobs maintain a sense of balance in their lives. They need to be reminded not to neglect families, friends, or themselves. (Dr. Papalia has summarized his outplacement experience with Smith Corona in a small booklet: An Inside Look at Outplacement Counseling.)

LESSONS LEARNED FROM OUTPLACEMENT PRACTICE AND EXPERIENCE

Gerald Bush
Heller School, Brandeis University

Over the last 10 years the highly visible downsizing in many industries has brought media attention to the professional outplacement industry. Claims for the first commercial outplacement activity, however, occurred in the early 1960s. By the second half of the 1960s the outplacement industry was clearly established with the formation of companies such as Challenger, Gray and Christmas in Chicago, Drake Beam and Associates and THInc, in New York City. THInc was the first specialized senior executive outplacement firm, and Drake Beam and Associates did the first group outplacement in 1969. The Association of Outplacement Consulting Firms was established in 1979 (Meyer and Shadle, 1994). In the 1990s, many large private sector employers have developed (often in conjunction with professional outplacement firms) their own models for the outplacement process. Examples of these employers include AT&T, General Electric, IBM, and Chemical Bank.

The purpose of this paper is to review the lessons of some 30 years of outplacement experience. The paper follows the temporal course of outplacement from planning and notification through termination and job search, focusing on the techniques and processes used by employers to implement outplacement. In following the outplacement process, the paper focuses on the techniques and processes used by employers and discusses the needs of the employees who are impacted by these processes, especially those who become candidates for job search.

The Decisions to Downsize

Outplacement experience stresses three major objectives that need to be considered when the organization first thinks about downsizing: the long-term, sustainable success of the organization, the well-being of employees who are leaving, and the well-being of employees who are staying.

One lesson learned from outplacement experience is foremost: downsizing should be planned, be executed, and be over with. The worst thing that can happen from the point of view of the organization, of those still employed, and of those being terminated is an announcement of "final" layoffs, followed by the news that there are more layoffs to come. Faced with such conflicting information, all employees will believe, rightly or wrongly, that their jobs are in jeopardy. It is best for the organization and for all its employees to do it [downsize], do it right, and do it quickly.

The Elements of a Downsizing and Outplacement Plan

There are four major steps in planning an organizational downsizing or closing (see box). The first and most critical step is: Determine the Future Desired State—that is, anticipate what the organization will look like after the decision to close or downsize has been implemented. If the situation is a total closing, this is relatively simple. However, even in these cases, parts of the organization may be relocated. Clarity and certainty regarding all aspects of the downsizing (organization structure, function and personnel) are critical.

The second step is: Assess the Present State—to clarify all aspects of the current situation. Planners must get up-to-date information on the numbers, age, gender, years of service, work records, and skills of the current workforce, which includes both active employees and employees on leave.

The third step is: Compare the Future and Present State—which requires analyzing what achieving the future desired state will do for the overall organization. This is the detailed answer to the question, "Why are we taking this trip?" Answers are usually expressed first in terms of strategic mission and goals and then in terms of more quantitative objectives such as cost savings, increases in productivity, adjustments to environmental changes, and the like. In addition, comparisons of current work processes and how they will be affected by downsizing are extremely important. These comparisons are necessary to detail which activities and people will stay, and which will be transferred or terminated. Organizations that neglect this step of planning run the risk of announcing terminations and then being forced to recall people because essential work must be done. This is, at best, bad management and, at worst, inhumane treatment. It is also important for the organization to consider how good (unbiased) its performance evaluation systems are and to make decisions about the role that performance evaluation ratings will play in deciding which people will be asked to leave. An organization that does not deal with the role of performance evaluations in downsizing will be vulnerable to lawsuits from disgruntled displaced workers and may suffer from the lowered morale of employees still on board.

The fourth step is to determine the "How?" and "When?" of the process and involves planning the implementation of the downsizing or closing. Answers to these questions may seem among the most straightforward in the planning process. However, like many things in life, success

Steps in Planning Downsizing

1. Determine the Future Desired State
2. Assess the Present State
3. Compare the Future and Present State by Answering the Question: "What Will Achieving the Future Desired State Do for the Organization?"
4. Answer the Questions: How? When?

in planning and implementing a downsizing is in the details, which include:

- designing new work processes and being ready to implement them at the time of downsizing;
- designing new reporting relationships and being ready to implement them immediately;
- deciding, in advance, on promotions or demotions that will occur in the newly configured organization;
- assigning relatively easy work to remaining employees the first few weeks following layoffs and then providing challenging assignments;
- talking with suppliers and customers within the first few hours or days of downsizing to reduce apprehension and ensure that quality relationships are maintained;
- developing contingency plans in the event of a work stoppage;
- developing contingency plans in the event of violence or threats of violence;
- scheduling sessions with employees who are staying to explain the need for the closing, downsizing, or realignment and related terminations; discuss their reactions and future career prospects with them; discuss ways in which they can relate to and support friends who are leaving;
- making certain that there are adequate financial and human resources to maintain the downsizing work and its accompanying psychological, physical, and administrative burdens;
- having the layoff plan reviewed by knowledgeable outsiders to make certain that the plan represents best practice and conforms to all relevant state or federal laws;
- having all public announcements and plans for public relations, especially those released to the local community, prepared and managed by knowledgeable staff;

• providing training to people who will be doing the exit interviews; and

• providing support systems to employees who will be staying and those who will be leaving.

Organizational downsizing or closing needs to be managed by a team of people qualified to deal with the multitude of issues that arise throughout the process. A task force of competent persons should be created as early in the process as possible. For sizable closing or downsizing efforts, such a task force or team should include benefits experts, career development and training specialists, financial analysts, real estate experts, operations management experts, and operating management.

Implementing Downsizing

Once the major steps in planning downsizing are completed, implementation of these plans begins. The first step in implementation is the announcement of downsizing and terminations. Typically there is a general announcement about downsizing and terminations made to the organization's entire workforce, followed by announcements to the press. Group meetings may be held with the employees to be terminated to provide some additional details about the reasons for downsizing and the conditions of termination. At this stage of the termination process, the employees will be in shock, and the employer should not expect any significant recall of the details of the meetings. These meetings should be augmented by exit interviews with each terminating employee.

Termination Announcements and Timing

The timing of termination announcements is also important. Many organizations are legally compelled to provide 60 to 90 days notification of impending terminations. This advance notification, although resisted by many organization, leads to employees perceiving the termination process as being fairer and also helps employees prepare themselves for their job search. Some organizations have provided as much as 18 to 24 months notification without suffering negative consequences, such as lower morale, decreased productivity, and workplace conflict. There is no good rule of thumb about the optimal length of advance notice, but longer periods are apparently not so risky as many employers have believed them to be.

The Termination Interview

The primary objective of a termination interview is to make certain the employee realizes that his or her dismissal is a business decision that is final and irrevocable. In a word, the employment contract is broken and reemployment will not occur in the foreseeable future. (Although reemployment is possible, reemployment rights and conditions should be clearly spelled out.)

A major conclusion gleaned from outplacement industry experience is that people conducting the termination or exit interviews must be trained to do them. The organization cannot assume that the average supervisor has the required interview skills. Indeed, outplacement professionals routinely share horror stories of employees leaving termination interviews thinking that they were just promoted, that they have another year or more on the job, or that their supervisors loved firing them. There are even reports of supervisors who tell their secretaries to "do the deed." A second step in implementing terminations is thus training the supervisors who will be handling exit interviews.

The training for exit or termination interviews should prepare supervisors to give employees the business-related reason(s) for their dismissal. The reasons for the downsizing should be presented in outline form and in a concise manner (no more than three minutes) and made as specific as possible to the particular employee's job.

Supervisors should also be prepared to give employees any necessary severance data. These should include details on salary continuation (if any), the status of health and dental insurance, payments for vacation and/or sick days not used, the continuation and/or conversion of life insurance, unemployment insurance entitlement and starting dates, pension entitlement and elections, if any, and all other benefits information. If relevant, reemployment rights should also be spelled out. Supervisors must also cover the details on how and when the employee is to exit the organization. This involves vacating office space, returning vehicles, turning in identification badges and keys, credit cards, and the like. The last day the person is expected to report for work should be specified. Information on severance and check-out details is best communicated when it is prepared in writing individually for each employee. A written document enables the employee to review termination benefits and last day of work details privately, with time to plan.

Outplacement experts suggest that exit or termination interviews take place on a Tuesday or Wednesday morning. A Friday afternoon interview can result in a weekend of potential pain, brooding, disorientation, contemplation of lawsuits, and other possibly destructive thoughts and behaviors. The midweek timing allows for an orderly exit during the regular business week. It can also encourage employees to use some time during that week to start thinking about the preliminaries of a job search.

Finally, supervisors should be trained to use the termination interview to express organizational regrets about the need to downsize and concern about the departing employee. Conveying this message is key to helping employees preserve positive attitudes and is essential for maintaining their self-esteem. One concrete means of expressing the organization's concern is the offer of a letter of reference. If the termination is "no-fault," there should be no problem in preparing a "To Whom It May Concern" letter that includes: dates of employment, job titles held, duties performed, merit recognitions given, a sentence covering reasons for termination, and the name and address of a person who could be contacted for elaboration. A copy of the letter could be given to the person during the termination interview. (Note: the employer should make all decisions regarding reference policy before the terminations are announced. The person doing the exit interview must know and communicate the policy clearly and accurately.) Obviously, the severance package is the most powerful tool the employer has to demonstrate willingness to help a departing employee. The second most powerful tool is the level of concern conveyed by the supervisor conducting the exit interview.

The message of concern is also important because of its impact on employees left behind. If survivors feel that dismissals were handled fairly and justly, it will show in their attitude and work. If the opposite is true, it will also show.

Supporting Job Loss

Employers must understand that in addition to being a financial event, the loss of a job is a complex psychological, physiological, and social event for individuals. Experience shows that people often respond mentally to job loss with increased anxiety or depression, lowered self-esteem, more abuse of drugs or alcohol, and even suicidal thoughts. Increases in psychosomatic illnesses have been documented with job loss: headaches, sleep and eating problems, and fatigue. An increase in more serious health problems is not uncommon: more high blood pressure, heart, and gastrointestinal problems.

From a social viewpoint, job loss can affect family and friends negatively. Spouses may experience many of the same mental and physical health problems that the laid-off worker does. Family discord and conflict or abuse can increase. A displaced worker can also lose contact or common interests with many of his or her friends as a result of job loss.

The result is social isolation and increased difficulty in pursuing the interactions with people that can help find a new job. A worker's social circle tends to grow smaller the longer unemployment persists.

The social costs of job loss for the larger community are well documented. In addition to the lowered morale of surviving coworkers, there is typically some downturn in demand for many business products and services in the community. In the case of major downsizing, this may lead to lowered economic vitality for the entire community. Given the increase in family conflicts and mental and physical health problems, there will also be an increased demand for community social and security services—demands that these services may not be adequately prepared to meet. At minimum, advance warning of a downsizing or closing and perhaps some financial resources should be given to local human service agencies. Employers should also actively inform potential job sources about the scope of their downsizing plans. Notice should be given to local employment assistance agencies— public and private. Efforts should be made to contact other employers, formal and informal support groups, the state employment service, and other possible employment sources. The employer's purpose in informing employment sources is to "weave a web of supports and community involvement (AOCFI, 1994)." In fact, an attempt should be made to create partnerships with all possible sources of social and employment support in the community.

Employers also need to understand that individual reactions to job loss vary. For example, some people tend to view themselves as having more control over their lives and will have more resilience and energy than others in dealing with setbacks such as job loss. Individuals will also differ in their financial resources, in their interests in alternative careers or retraining, and in their other life goals (such as early retirement) at the time of job loss. Demographic factors are relevant, too, such as level of education, age, gender, race/ethnicity, and marital status. For example, single mothers with little education and limited financial resources may find job loss more traumatic than highly educated, married women whose spouses have well-paid jobs.

Finally, situational factors can influence the stress individuals experience with job loss. The economic environment is important. If unemployment in the area is generally high, this tends to make workers feel more discouraged about the area labor market and getting another good job. This feeling will be even stronger when the general economic conditions in the country are viewed as negative. In addition, the nature of the worker's attachment to the organization and the type of layoff or downsizing situation occurring will affect reactions to job loss. Reactions to job loss may be more intense for employees who believe they have secure, career-long "psychological contracts" with their employers and who are faced with the permanent loss of their jobs.

Many government employers, for example, have offered such long-term psychological contracts to employees. People who sought government employment have often been willing to accept lower pay, a more bureaucratic work life, and the possibility of transfers in exchange for work that has national importance (or at least serves the public interest), and for career progress and overall job security that are protected by government personnel systems. Most government employees believed that if they worked diligently their employment contract was secure. In many government jobs, job security has been the rule for so long, that when employees are faced with involuntary termination they react with greater feelings of shock, disbelief, betrayal, and even violation than employees with less secure 'psychological' employment contracts might.

Understanding individual reactions to job loss helps employers understand the need to expand outplacement programs and practices beyond a focus on getting a job. The fact that job loss is stressful and can result in financial, psychological, physical, and social problems means that employers should consider programs that provide some support in each of these areas. Financial support can come through severance pay, medical benefit extensions, financial counseling, and assistance in finding community sources of funds for welfare, retraining, and relocation. Emotional, physical, and social support can come through the provision of counseling and health services, as well as through the structure of support groups and formal centers where people can gather for workshops and conduct their job searches. The fact that individuals vary in their reactions to job loss depending on personality and demographic and situational factors means that employers need to consider a full range of outplacement options—retraining, career counseling, retirement counseling, relocation, geographically wide-ranging job leads, self-employment, etc., and allow individuals some discretion in the time it takes to find a new job or another alternative.

Supporting the Job Search

Outplacement experience suggests that employers can support individuals in their search for new jobs by:

- providing some formal structure for the search—a support group, a central location for information, or a formal outplacement center, and an outplacement process to follow;
- offering some support in assessing current skills and identifying skill gaps that, if filled, may increase employment opportunities.

• offering training and education that covers cultural and technical aspects of potential new jobs, as well as specific workshops on job search skills; and

• coordinating information on jobs, training, and other funds from community agencies, businesses, and placement sources.

In providing a formal structure for job search, the employer recognizes that most employees have lost the formal structure that work demands place on their time. Ideally, a center devoted to job search can be set up somewhere off the work site. This center is a place where outplaced employees can regularly report, see others, and maintain a sense of purpose in pursuing their job searches. If such a center is not possible, then the employer can be instrumental in setting up support groups or job clubs, providing employees with ideas about how to set up their own job search "command central" at home, or setting up an organizational help line to support individuals in getting appointments with community training, mental health, and employment counselors.

A sense of purpose and process in outplacement is also important for employers to establish. Employees entering outplacement need to understand that it is a process that starts with grieving the job loss, getting support, assessing career goals and interests, defining job goals, writing a resume, searching, interviewing, and so forth. Finding a job is hard work and individuals must work at it as hard as they would at a regular job.

Employers should use their resources to identify likely sources of employment locally, regionally, and nationally for people with the skills they are outplacing. This may require conducting surveys or analyzing existing ones, hiring experts to develop this information, buying access rights to major electronic job databases, and other forms of networking with industry and social contacts. Although such information is often difficult for employers to obtain, it is nearly impossible for individuals to get otherwise. At the same time, this information is crucial to outplaced employees' decisions on which skills to upgrade or acquire and how much time to invest in this process.

Effective outplacement includes opportunities for several different kinds of training and education. Technical training to develop or upgrade specific job skills is one type. Outplacement programs can direct employees to the best sources for such training and help them find funding. Education about cultural changes related to the new employment contract and the transformed workplace is another type of training that needs to be part of outplacement offerings. Employees need to understand work options such as contract or project work, self-employment, placement internships, and so forth. Many individuals want to find another "permanent" job, but changes in the workplace may make this unlikely. Even "permanent" jobs may include flexible work assignments and self-directed teams that individuals may not know from their previous jobs.

Employers need to include a variety of experiential workshops designed to develop job search skills, including resume writing, interviewing, how to develop job leads (networking and informational interviewing), and how to handle rejection. Workshops should emphasize that job candidates must market themselves according to employers' needs.

Finally, the organization's outplacement efforts should include coordination and centralization of information from a variety of sources helpful to job search. These include community educational providers, sources of government funding for training and living expenses, job opportunities from local, regional, and national sources, unemployment benefits services, etc. Ideally, the success or failure of different ways to develop job leads, different sources of job information, the usefulness of local workshops and programs, and feedback from employers using the outplacement service would also be part of the information shared for the benefit of people searching for jobs and the organization funding outplacement.

Conclusion

Among the foremost lessons learned during 30 years of outplacement experience is that effective outplacement requires planning when downsizing is still only a glimmer in the top management team's vision. Organizations must be able to articulate what downsizing will mean to the workforce—why downsizing is necessary, who will be affected, and how they will be affected. The ability to be so articulate about downsizing often requires the appointment of a downsizing team that represents all the line and staff interests and expertise that will be involved throughout the process. Planning and communications about downsizing will affect both employees who stay and those who leave. In particular, the people conducting termination and exit interviews for employees being outplaced must be trained in what information to provide *and* in how to provide it.

Outplacement experience also suggests that departing employees need assistance in coping with job loss. Counseling, either in-house or by referral to the community, is needed to help employees work through the negative feelings and actions that often accompany job loss. The fact that individuals will vary in their reactions to job loss and in their interest in finding alternatives requires that outplacement efforts include a variety of options—training, self-employment, retirement, relocation, and career planning. Negative reactions to job loss also mean that the organization has a responsibility to coordinate downsizing with community businesses and a range of other service providers.

Finally, experience shows that outplacement efforts focused on helping individuals find jobs should provide structure (both in terms of place and process) for the job search; technical and cultural training relevant to the needs of today's workplace; and workshops on resume writing, interviewing, developing jobs, and handling rejections. These workshops are most effective when they allow employees to role play, practice, and get direct feedback on their job search skills. Employers should coordinate information on sources of jobs, funding, and other information relevant to job search and make it available to outplaced employees. Details on what is working or not working will both help job searchers and improve employer outplacement efforts.

Bibliography

Allen, Jeffrey G.
1992 *The Perfect Follow-up Method to Get the Job.* New York: John Wiley.
Asher, Donald
1995 *The Foolproof Job-Search Workbook.* Berkeley, CA: Ten Speed Press.
Association of Outplacement Consulting Firms International (AOCFI)
1994 *Final Report to the U.S. Department of Labor.* Washington, DC: U.S. Department of Labor.
AT&T
1994 *With Respect to People.* Morristown, NJ: AT&T.
Bolles, Richard Nelson.
1996 *The 1996 What Color Is Your Parachute.* Berkeley, CA: Ten Speed Press.
Bridges, William
1991 *Managing Transitions.* Reading, MA: Addison-Wesley Publishing Company.
Buron, William J., S.J.
1995 *Finding Work Without Losing Heart.* Holbrook, MA: Adams Publishing.
Gottlieb, Marvin R., and Lori Conkling.
1995 *Managing the Workplace Survivors.* Westport, CT: Quorum Books.
Meyer, John L., and Carolyn C. Shadle
1994 *The Changing Outplacement Process.* Westport, CT: Quorum Books.
Morin, William J., and Lyle Yorks
1990 *Dismissal: There Is No Easy Way But There Is A Better Way.* New York: Harcourt Brace Jovanovich.
Noer, David N.
1993 *Healing The Wounds: Overcoming the Trauma of Layoffs and Revitalizing Downsized Organizations.* San Francisco: Jossey-Bass Publishers.
Papalia, Anthony S.
1995 *An Inside Look at Outplacement Counseling: The Relocation of Smith-Corona to Mexico.* Cortland, NY: Cortland Press.
Pickman, Alan J.
1994 *Complete Guide To Outplacement Counseling.* Hillsdale, NJ: Lawrence Erlbaum Associates.

REMARKS

Jack Ryan
Manager of Recruitment, Placement, and Employment Practices
General Electric Aircraft

General Electric (GE) is a diversified, global manufacturing and service company in 12 businesses. We are number one or two in our respective industries—or, following Jack Welch's vision, we fix, close, or sell the business. Organizationally, we are committed to customer satisfaction via speed and quality production and service. This commitment has meant that we drive decision making and accountability to the lowest levels possible; we have reduced layers of management and downsized considerably over the last five years. GE has developed a general model for outplacement that is tailored to the business using it. I will be focusing on outplacement that has occurred at GE Aircraft in Cincinnati, Ohio. One "best practice warning": the data I will share with you has worked at GE Aircraft but, as Peter Senge said in *The Fifth Discipline*, if we rely totally on best practices, the Wright Brothers would have never flown.

Between 1992 and 1995, GE Aircraft ran two transition centers, one for professional and one for hourly employees. In 1995, as the volume of outplacement declined, these two centers were combined. The centers are both off-site and at the peak of outplacement served 300 or more transitioning employees daily. We hired expert center managers, roughly one for each 25-30 participants. The centers were fully resourced, that is, there were ample private workstations, long distance telephone services, on-line job search services, national newspapers, information on job fairs, labor market job postings, and kid play areas. We believe that full resourcing of the transition centers makes a statement to employees about how much you care about them. One-stop shopping is a center feature. All services that participants might need—all types of counseling, federal program assistance, etc.—are in one location. Our centers have served about 4,000 people, or 65 percent of the total number of GE Aircraft employees downsized over the last four years.

The GE outplacement model suggests that each business define a mission, values, and general operating principles for its outplacement practices. At GE Aircraft this suggestion was translated as: offering world-class transition assistance that achieves reemployability for participants and treats them with dignity and fairness. Center operations were planned prior to downsizing, and communications about downsizing were provided to all parties concerned—workers, managements, families, and labor representatives. The centers were staffed by experts, and programs were designed to be flexible enough to meet the different and changing needs of participants.

The transition process at GE Aircraft involved 60 days notice of job loss. Upon notification, employees were encouraged to think that their new job was finding a job. On-site orientation sessions were held for groups of employees shortly after notification to inform them about counseling services, their outplacement benefits packages, and the range of services offered at the transition centers. Families were encouraged to tour the centers. Following on-site orientation, employees could sign up for transition center services: two 4-hour job search workshops covering counseling, testing and career guidance, and information on how to prepare resumes, organize for a job search, interview, etc. Each participant could also get 3 hours of individual counseling and coaching related to job searches (mock interviews, videos of interview style, resume finalization, and how to negotiate for a job). Employees could use the center up to 2 years after their notification.

We have learned some key lessons in 4-plus years of outplacement at GE Aircraft. Probably the most critical lesson is that job development is essential to effective reemployment of outplaced employees. We hired experts to go out and canvass local, regional, and national work opportunities for employees with different skills and then bring information on these openings back to the transition centers. These experts identified the top 10 hiring companies in our region, found out what kind of people they were hiring, and used this information to drive workshops and direct center participants to training. We estimate that this approach to job development secured one-third of the jobs found by our salaried center participants. It is interesting to note that the hourly employees who participated at the hourly transition center had less difficulty in finding jobs than our professional and managerial employees. This is probably due to the nature of the local labor market and the relatively strong demand for hourly workers. Our local unions were also active in scouting jobs.

A second lesson learned is that training managers in how to do exit interviews is critical. When you sit facing an employee who has given heart and soul to the company for 15 or more years, who has three kids in college, and you have to explain to them some rationale for eliminating his or her job—it's a momentous task. Managers need tools and coaching to do it, including where to do the interview, what to say first, the exact content of the message, what different reactions to expect, and how to handle them. No matter what other communications have been directed to departing employees, the exit interview is where the shoe drops. You've got to be sure employees understand that this is final.

Another lesson learned is the importance of helping survivors, the employees who are not leaving. You know, my friend of 15 years has been laid off; he lives next door to me; I'm the godfather of his kids. How do I handle this? Is my job next? We ask that survivors use our employee assistance program for counseling about these feelings.

A fourth lesson learned involves the importance of up-front planning. Outplacement planning should coincide with planning for downsizing. We got experts involved early on in the process; we worked with a joint management and labor committee early on in the process. Both efforts paid off. On the downside, and in hindsight, we believe we should have marketed employee participation in the transition centers more heavily from the outset of downsizing. For example, we could have done benchmarking of other centers within GE and advertised the fact that people who use the centers are X percent more likely to find jobs than people who don't. We could have worked with the state unemployment services earlier on to say that employees must use either the transition centers or the state's workshops if they want to collect their unemployment benefits. We should have had fully operational transition centers ready when outplacing started, but the start-up date was delayed. All these things meant lower center participation than we would have liked.

Finally, we learned that we should have tracked participant demographics and center use and reemployment data better. This would have made it much easier to say which activities were resulting in jobs for which participants. We started doing some tracking of data for our professional and managerial center participants and found that, of about 1,700 employees, 80 percent found new jobs, 10 percent moved or couldn't be contacted, 5 percent went back to school, 1 percent retired, 3 percent started their own businesses, and 1 percent chose to stay home. Of the participants who found jobs, 88 percent found jobs locally. We need to manage outplacement to deal with all these choices. We also need data to know when and if to wind down outplacement operations.

Susan Diamond
Senior Career Management Professional, Right Associates, and Director, Mobil Research and Development Career Center

Right Associates is the largest and fastest-growing firm of its kind, specializing in human resources consulting and outplacement services. We have 131 offices worldwide and our clients include 400 of the *Fortune* 500. Right Associates has considerable experience in providing workshops on retirement, career planning, and outplacement to military and civilian personnel at over 50 Army bases and a few other sites, including ships at sea.

To give you a snapshot of reemployment in the private sector, I'd like to share with you results from a sample of over 14,000 individuals in

Right Associates full-service programs over the past 10 years. Full service is defined as one-on-one career counseling, office space, and administrative support for 6 to 12 months. The most significant result from this sample is that virtually all people from all skill backgrounds were reemployed within their severance periods: 81 percent were employed in new jobs; 19 percent were self-employed. (Our full-service programs include assistance to those who want self-employment; we work with them to develop a viable business plan.) Of this sample, 60 percent earned plus or minus 10 percent of what they were previously earning. However, some wanted to change their lifestyles and pursue a new career. Right Associates believes it is important to not only help people find jobs, but also to help them achieve career satisfaction as they define it. For example, just last week, a client who, at the initial stages of the outplacement process, was one of the most angry and bitter I had ever encountered, came by to thank us because we helped him transform what he once regarded as a fantasy—work that indulged his love of roller coasters—into a realistic job objective. Though he was skeptical about our process, we pushed him into networking with roller coaster organizations—yes, they do exist. As a result, he has been hired as a design engineer for a theme park in Florida. Such results, much more so than placement in a high-paying job, define career satisfaction for me.

We have already learned a lot from our morning panelists (the commissioned paper authors and Amiram Vinokur) and from Jack Ryan of GE, about career centers or transition centers, the principles on which they operate, and the types of services they offer. I would like to reinforce some of the information they have provided and also highlight some of our experiences that are particularly important. I am also recommending two books that should probably be collectively subtitled "everything you ever wanted to know about termination but were afraid to ask." The first is *Essential Facts: Termination of Employment* by Richard Chagnon; the second is *Lessons Learned: Dispelling the Myths of Downsizing* by Right Associates.

As to our experience. First, I'd like to reinforce Amiram Vinokur's remarks about the importance of active learning in job search workshops. Our consultants view themselves as facilitators who draw out what a person already knows and provide positive feedback to increase motivation and self-esteem. Second, should career services be customized to different skills levels or types of employees? Yes and no. Yes, democracy rules when it comes to access to physical resources and community services such as state unemployment services and federal program counselors. No, when it comes to counseling, workshops, training, career guidance, networking teams, etc. Content, job examples, pacing, and even vocabulary need to be tailored to the skill group and level of the clients.

Common sense alone dictates that counseling for a chief executive officer will differ from counseling for an information science professional. Ideally you separate and serve different groups, but sometimes you must deal with mixed groups. In the latter case, you have to make sure that junior-level people are not intimidated by the senior levels.

Third, our experience dictates that at our centers we must focus on training for which we are particularly qualified. For example, we do not teach people to read, although we will diagnose their need for such training. Instead, we send them to vocational programs in the area, and professionals in literacy provide instruction. We do, however, teach people how to use the Internet to find job opportunities: posting resumes, accessing relevant job listings, and so forth. Right Associates has developed software that enables people to identify their skills and match them with *Dictionary of Occupational Titles* equivalents. This same software can help them find data on additional educational requirements for these equivalents, where to go for more training, expected earnings, and employment prospects, etc. A warning on Internet use: we emphasize that the Internet is only one way to find jobs and not more likely than other ways to secure jobs. We ask our clients to spend no more than 10 to 12 percent of their search time on Internet. People can get addicted to using it.

Our clients can also use Right Associates software to highlight the names of employers in their geographic area who have indicated an interest in hiring people with their skills. These are employers that Right Associates has identified through job development activities. The Right Associates proprietary system, Job Bank, contains about 7,000 job listings at any point in time. In addition, we use telemarketers to actively market job candidates. These types of activities help develop networks if not actual job prospects.

Reinforcing remarks Leaetta Hough (commissioned paper author) made this morning, Right Associates uses a lot of self-assessment materials to measure interests, skills, communications styles, personality type, and so forth. Also, as she suggested, we make sure that each person knows how to use this information to help define career goals and job objectives. We emphasize that no matter who your former employer was (for example, the military), you need to market yourself in ways that prospective employers can understand and fit into their organizations. Do not describe yourself as a bureaucrat with lots of furlough experience, but rather as someone who has specific administrative, systems, or decision-making skills that can be used in most organizations.

Finally, we focus on communications with employees in as many ways and formats as possible. One message we particularly emphasize is that we are teaching people to learn how to pursue lifetime employability, not lifetime employment.

I'd like to close with some brief remarks about selecting outplacement consultants and the type of relationship we at Right Associates believe it is important to develop with our clients. In selecting consultants, it is important to find people who have considerable training and experience in developing jobs, in tailoring programs to client needs, who offer technological support, who establish performance criteria against which outplacement services can be judged, and who have the ability to work with your organization to do outplacement. I have already talked about Right Associates' abilities to do job development and its practice of tailoring programs to clients. We also set baseline metrics against which we can evaluate our programs for each organizational client. For example, we measure job development—how many leads come in and how many people get interviewed as a result. We also set measures for the performance of our center facilitators, workshop use and usefulness, relevance of workshop content, daily center usage, and so forth. We can add to these measures to meet the specific needs of an organization. Right Associates also has the organizational consulting expertise to work with our clients from the beginning of a restructuring or downsizing. For example, we can begin assisting with internal communications before the rumor mills get started. We can start the outplacement orientation process and work with survivors early on. We can help people begin the mental reframing and getting over the emotional hurdles that go along with the new employment contract. The military, believe me, does not have monopoly on a workforce that believes their jobs are an entitlement.

Finishing up, a very wise career development professor I had in graduate school said that he always gave open-book tests because life is an open-book test. I do not know all the answers, but I do subscribe to the open-book theory. I can put you in touch with people who do have answers or know where they can be found.

Ellen R. Jackson
Resource Link Director,
Corporate Human Resources Organization, AT&T

Right now AT&T is making headlines daily for its restructuring efforts. Today I'd like to tell you the rest of the story. I support an organization within AT&T called Resource Link, and I'd like to focus on this organization in my remarks this afternoon. Until very recently, I have supported AT&T's outplacement centers. We have seven of these nationwide, and over the past 4 years they have serviced about 25,000 people. Quite frankly, any comments I would make regarding these centers would just be echoing what we've already heard.

I need to give you some background on AT&T in order for you to understand the role Resource Link plays in the company. Currently AT&T is going through what we call a trivestiture. We are spinning off major pieces of our business, and this requires dramatic restructuring. Our mission, however, remains the same: to be the best at bringing the world's people together and give them access to one another anytime, anywhere. Our environment has changed dramatically with technological advances and changes in market regulation. Just two weeks ago, President Clinton signed the Telecommunications Act, which we anticipate will open up competition for us that we cannot right now really fathom.

Nevertheless, many of the downsizing and outplacement practices we put in place in 1991 when we acquired NCR and began restructuring are still in place and have paid off. At that time, we anticipated not only major redundancies in our workforce, but also a need for more flexible employment arrangements that would help our workforce balance work and lifestyle needs and better accommodate cycles in labor demand.

Downsizing and outplacement planning went hand in hand with our thinking about restructuring. With regard to our internal labor markets, we have implemented a host of practices, including selected hiring freezes and reskilling efforts (managed jointly with the Communication Workers and the International Brotherhood of Electrical Workers) and opened seven freestanding career centers with satellite locations. These centers and their satellites open and close in response to outplacement needs. Center services are available for all departing employees, from executives to mailroom clerks.

We also established a number of programs that were designed to "buffer" demand cycles in our internal labor markets. For example, one of these programs is what we call a Special Leave of Absence Program (SELOA). The reasoning behind this programs is, "we do not need these folks today, but we may need them in a year or two." The SELOA program allows employees to volunteer to take up to 2 years leave of absence (in 6-month increments). AT&T will pay benefits during this absence and will reimburse tuition, following the same reimbursement rules that apply for all employees. You are guaranteed a job back at the end of the SELOA. We bridge accruals of pensions and seniority if employees come back, but not if they don't. The only restriction on employees who do not return is that they cannot go to work directly for one of our competitors. Thus far, nearly 5,000 people have taken advantage of this program. We lose about 40 percent of the employees who go on SELOA, but the others return refreshed and revitalized. We view the program as paying off in reduced severance pay, as a buffer, and as a means of showing employees that we care.

Resource Link, the organization that I direct, was conceived as another way to buffer the volatility of internal labor market demand. It allows us to maintain access to talent in which we have previously invested. We looked around and saw that we were already contracting services at the cost of more like $1 billion than $1 million. We also saw that there were definite matches between internal labor surpluses and the skills being contracted. Resource Link was designed to offer surplus employees a chance to offer their skills on a contract basis within AT&T. It is a business within a business. Resource Link runs as a P&L center with profit, customer satisfaction, and growth objectives. We have to be competitive because there is no requirement that AT&T customers choose us. Our profits are paid back to our clients as rebates.

Entry into Resource Link works like this: surplus employees can volunteer for Resource Link, but we also have to select them. We don't take all surplus employees, nor do all surplus employees volunteer. The point of entry into Resource Link is one of the career centers. So you have to have been given a 90-day notification and be enrolled in a career center in order to volunteer for Resource Link. We select about 10 to 15 percent of those who apply. People in Resource Link retain their AT&T pay once they have shown that they can get contract work within the company. There are two organizations within Resource Link—one for professional and managerial skills and the other (called Skills Match) for clerical and blue-collar skills. The personnel practices differ somewhat between the two. For example, Skills Match rules were negotiated with labor unions. Anyone at risk of being outplaced in clerical or blue-collar jobs is automatically enrolled in Skills Match and paid market rates for comparable contract workers.

Resource Link has been very successful. Last year we made $4 million profit and had an 85 percent contract renewal rate from our AT&T customers. We currently have 850 to 900 people or associates in our Resource Link talent pool. Just as important as our profit figures is that we believe our employees see Resource Link as highly visible evidence of our commitment to them. We are leaving no stone unturned in trying to find employment opportunities. At the same time, Resource Link makes more tangible the notion of the new employment contract. It is one way of reframing our psychological contract with our employees and responding to their requests to balance work and lifestyle demands with more flexibility.

Anne L. Messenger
Director, Employment Transition Center, Lockheed Martin

I plan to focus on my experience on best practices in outplacement. But I'll begin by recommending, no insisting, that you read two books. I am a reader; my office bookshelves are filled with books on outplacement how-tos and change management. The two books I am recommending have had the most powerful impact on me out of all those I have read. One is David Noer's book, *Healing the Wounds*. He begins the book with a powerful analogy for downsizing organizations. He describes a loving family (a mother, a father, and four children) who gather every morning for breakfast to discuss their lives. One morning the father and mother come to the table looking anxious and announce that they are suffering some financial difficulties and two of the children will have to go. The next morning the family meets for breakfast and two of the children are gone. There is no discussion of their absence; instead the parents talk about the picnic planned for Saturday and the need to do homework on time, and so forth. The relevance of this story for organizational survivors of downsizing is obvious; I don't need to elaborate.

The second book I recommend is William Bridges' *Job Shift*. I believe this book crystallized for me over a decade's worth of experience. The premise of the book is that work will always be with us. It is not going away. What is going away is the job, with its finite edges—9 to 5, five days a week, at your office, factory floor, or desk. There are lots of ways to make money if each of us can figure out how to do this, do it well, and, hopefully, do it happily.

Now to my experience. I have been doing outplacement for 11 years. Ten years ago there was no such word as *outplacement*—we had words like *dislocation, layoffs, firing, termination*. Now we have in addition to these, *downsizing, rightsizing, reengineering*, and *outplacement*. Outplacement is now a billion dollar industry. People have always been let go from their jobs in good ways and in bad ways. However, today the repeated media coverage makes even good layoffs sound bad. This is bad for the people being laid off and for the people who stay.

I have become a reluctant expert in the field of outplacement. When I began, there were no rules or guidelines. I was executive director of the Syracuse Onandaga County Private Industry Council. These councils oversee federally funded job training programs. Major layoffs in our small community hit hard, and our council was able to pull together and do a wonderful job of outplacement. We solicited and got federal funds for a worker reemployment center for the area, which was very successful in helping laid-off workers find new jobs. Today, I work with a major defense corporation that has gone through tremendous changes and acquisitions over the last 4 years. The contrast between doing outplacement with the private industry council and this relatively rich corporation is startling. I feel now as though I have comparatively unlimited support for the outplacement programs I want to offer.

Now, my views on outplacement. In my mind there are three major outplacement "musts." In outlining these, I am assuming that you have support from your top management to do outplacement—that is the first and foremost must. I am also assuming that you want to do a good job of outplacement, that interest in outplacement is not just lip service.

The first outplacement must: you must have crackerjack people involved in your outplacement efforts—intelligent, street smart, people smart, energetic, sensitive, gentle, but also tough enough to tell people what they need to do to get a job. You need people who can tell an engineer or a high-level manager to stop working on a resume for eight hours a day and get out on the streets to network and deliver the resume. I am firm about hiring outplacement center staff with a sense of humor and personal experience with layoffs. In addition to an excellent staff, you need quick access to people such as employee assistance program counselors, security people for protection, and charity people for social and welfare services. This is all to say that people have a lot more going on in their lives than the layoff. You may have people going through a divorce, or someone whose wife just found out she has cancer, or another who is suicidal or who decides to get a gun and start driving. You have to have resources waiting in the wings to help deal with such experiences.

The second outplacement must is connectedness—with your community, among your center staff, with your immediate clients at the center, and with the organization paying for the center services. There are several things that contribute to connectedness. One is that the center staff be trained, preferably at the center where they will work and with the people they will be working with. It is important that staff like one another, interact well together, and have a sense of humor about what the day brings. You do not want your center to have the atmosphere of a morgue. The center should also look good physically. This helps both staff and clients feel good about using it; it makes them feel important.

Another way to achieve connectedness is to continually market your center and maintain good relations with people in the community. This includes not only agencies like the United Way and Job Training Partnership Act offices, but also all the potential employers and training institutions. At my center we have a steady influx of community people coming in to do workshops, seminars, and so forth.

Finally, to achieve connectedness with clients, it is important to maintain communications. For example, we send newsletters to the center client's families. If the staff doesn't see someone at the center for several days, we'll give them a call. We use former clients and current clients in center activities whenever possible. We are in the middle of a move right now—transferring center services to another location—and I am using several client drafters without current jobs to help with the logistics and facilities planning. We have parties and ask former clients to come. Clients need this contact in order to stay motivated through the inevitable rejections they'll get in any job search.

My third and last outplacement must: you need to have good services and resources at the center. In my view, even more important than material resources is establishing a sense of place. The folks using your center have just lost their jobs. They need a place to socialize, a place to come, a place to work. We work hard to make people feel that the center is their new workplace where their job is to find a job. We are firm about sending the message that we are not going to do this job for them, and we expect them to do it full time, but when they leave the center they should get on with their lives. Go bowling, play with your kids. Then come back next day and do your job again fresh.

Workshops are an important service. They not only convey information but also provide a structure for the job search. We have an introductory workshop, and then a host of different workshops that people can select. We also insist that everyone go through counseling for at least one hour. The most important workshop in my view, after the initial introduction and counseling, is the one devoted to preparing a resume. Somehow, this helps people put all their jumble of ideas in some order and enhances self-esteem. Self-assessment is next, especially assessment designed to describe skills in language that prospective employers can understand. I guarantee you that everyone has transferrable skills. Links to training institutions or agencies such as the Job Training Partnership Act program are important resources for any center. Other important resources are word processing, clerical support, message services, and so forth.

To sum up, I told you I was going to share what I've learned in my 11 years of outplacement experience. I guess one of the most important things is that you can teach someone how to search for a job. I really think that is kind of mechanical. Teaching people to change their mental set is much more difficult. You can tell people about the new employment contract and the job shift. You can tell them what this means in terms of marketing themselves, upgrading skills, dealing with more financial unpredictability. But getting to this new mental set is hard. Three and one-half years ago I became a contractor. I went from a regular paycheck to a paycheck that I thought was enormous until I paid my first quarterly estimated tax. People need to hear about the new employment contract often and as early on as possible.

Anthony S. Papalia
Director, Student Development and Counseling,
State University of New York, Cortland, and
Outplacement Specialist, Smith Corona Corporation

I want to share some general principles about outplacement that I have learned in 20 years of workplace experience. I will focus on strategies that have not been emphasized by earlier presenters. For example, organizations must put in place an increased security system during major downsizing. Increased security should not only be placed at the main work facilities but also extended to the homes of key executives. This is not being an alarmist. There is a wide range of reaction to terminations, including violence.

The manner in which the initial announcement of termination is handled is important. Adequate support and security should be on location in advance of the termination announcement. Arrangement should be made to notify people who are absent from work about termination at the same time everyone else hears about it. Individuals in the workplace may become ill or disoriented at the news of termination and may require medical attention or transportation home.

Employees should not be told individually by their supervisor of their termination. Most supervisors are not equipped to deal with the diverse reactions that are likely to occur. Impacted workers should be gathered into manageable groups in which a brief prepared statement is read. The statement should be prepared and rehearsed well in advance of the presentation. At the conclusion of the statement, direction and information on outplacement services should be provided orally and in writing. Ideally employees should be paid for their initial outplacement attendance, generally a 2- or 3-day period.

If employees are entitled to a 60-day notice under the Worker Adjustment and Notification Act (WARN), human resource benefits specialists should meet with workers individually or in small groups to elaborate verbally and in writing on all worker rights and benefits, including health benefits, retirement options, severance packages, and financial planning.

It is important to recognize that people will be numb after they are told about the loss of their jobs. They are likely to forget most of what they were told in the termination announcement, thus the need to present the information in a variety of formats.

If education or retraining benefits are available to the dislocated workers, planning and counseling should begin as early as possible. Some education programs, such as nursing, offer entry into the program only once a year. Most higher education programs lack flexibility in program start up. Entry is usually limited to the beginning of an academic semester. The use of education fairs to inform workers on programs, options, and deadlines has proved very useful.

Individuals enrolled in short-term retraining programs were less successful in sustaining themselves in the workplace than those individuals enrolled in education programs of a year or two in duration. Training becomes obsolete, whereas education gives flexibility and stability.

Long-established firms engaged in downsizing or closure will surface large numbers of employees without high school diplomas. This became apparent in the Smith-Corona relocation to Mexico. Many dislocated employees felt they had a job for life and saw no need to complete a high school diploma. General Education Development classes were conducted for a 2-year period to provide dislocated workers the opportunity to earn a high school diploma and to qualify for retraining or further education programs.

In rural settings, the community needs to be involved in outplacement. Community involvement around the Smith Corona shutdown was intense. After community rallies aimed at preventing plant closure were unsuccessful, a meeting of over 25 community resource people was convened at the Smith Corona plant to form an outplacement steering committee. It included bankers, debt counselors, college personnel, mental health specialists, hospital representatives, public utility representatives, Chamber of Commerce executives, local employers, state Department of Labor specialists, area private industry councils, and area educational and social service members. This committee mobilized community resources to assist the dislocated workers in a variety of ways. Financial and debt counseling services were particularly critical in helping employees deal with large severance payments, mortgage refinancing, utility payments, and retirement planning. Alternative medical coverages were of great concern along with their affordability. Families with children in college needed special assistance to deal with college costs and the adjustment of financial aid programs in progress.

The outplacement steering committee coordinated with government agencies to get all the dislocation and training assistance possible for workers leaving Smith Corona. The committee conducted surveys of both departing workers and local employers to identify job opportunities and match them with worker skills. Both training and job fairs were sponsored as a part of committee efforts to introduce workers to local resources for information on jobs and training. Smith Corona also worked closely with the state unemployment service. Their network of job opportunities helped direct the dislocated workers in their job search outside of the community. This was especially important in finding jobs for hourly workers who generally had less experience in searching for jobs, less interest in relocating, and more need for skill upgrading than many professional and managerial workers. The expertise of Job Service Trade Adjustment Assistance and TRA specialists enabled workers to receive over $1.5 million in education and retraining benefits that resulted in a better trained workforce to attract new industries.

Dislocated workers with high skill levels had interest in starting small business operations. Assistance was rendered by the Small Business Administration and the Senior Corps of Retired Executives. The Senior Corps of Retired Executives offered information and consultation at no cost to individuals seeking to start their own businesses.

In closing I would stress it is essential to help dislocated workers establish and maintain a sense of balance in their lives. Critical incident stress debriefing sessions proved to be effective in helping workers establish balance in their life while working through the grief of job loss.

PART III
The Department of Defense Outplacement Task

The task now facing the Department of Defense, the "one-third to go," mentioned at the outset of these proceedings, will necessarily involve more involuntary terminations. It is an outplacement task of unprecedented scope and certainly a highly visible one. Of course the department has made plans and begun programs for outplacement. For example, the Departments of Defense and Labor have coordinated outplacement efforts by conducting joint, informational site visits to closing bases. These visits were designed to provide information and technical assistance to workers and community members relevant to the range of services and assistance available through federal and local Job Training Partnership Act (JTPA) programs. The site visits have been instrumental in getting JTPA and related funds for many base communities. The workshop papers, panel remarks, and discussions have generated a wealth of information that can be used by the Office of Civilian Personnel Policy. Some of it offers reassurance that the office's current thinking and practices are on the right track; some of it offers new ideas for fine-tuning current practices or initiating new ones.

A clearer picture of the outplacement task still facing the Department of Defense provides a better context for understanding the workshop ideas most relevant for its outplacement efforts. What are the demographics for those 119,000 civilian employees yet to be downsized?

As of September 1995, the total civilian population of the Department of Defense numbered 850,000. Three-fourths of this workforce is in white-collar occupations (professional, administrative, technical, and clerical), and the other fourth in blue-collar occupations. Nearly 40 percent of the workforce has between 11 and 20 years of service; another 22 percent has between 21 and 30 years of service. The majority of separations that have occurred to date have been among people with less than 10 years of service. Retirement and other separation incentives have had some impact on the number of retirements since downsizing began, but not enough to offset the bulge of people with more than 10 years of service who remain. Future outplacement efforts must target this high service group.

Current downsizing projections mean that at least 15 percent of this population of 850,000 will have to be outplaced. The civilian employment population at the 52 bases now designated for closure offers the clearest picture of the outplacement task over the next few years. There are approximately 85,000 civilian employees at these bases: 60 percent are in white-collar and 40 percent in blue-collar occupations. Only 20 percent are currently eligible for retirement. One-third of this workforce is female; 18 percent, black; 11 percent, Hispanic; and 7 percent, other (mostly Asian). The geographic distribution of the bases is heavily concentrated in just four states: California (26 percent of the workforce, 13 bases), Pennsylvania (12 percent of the workforce, 4 bases), Texas (10 percent of the workforce, 5 bases), and Tennessee (10 percent of the workforce, 1 base). The other 29 bases are scattered across 21 states.

Three bases account for nearly one-third of the civilian head count: the Defense Distribution Depot in Tennessee; Kelly Air Force Base in Texas; and McClelland Air Force Base in California. There is a high proportion of clerical and blue-collar workers and nearly 21 percent of all civilian black employees at the Defense Distribution Depot. Kelly Air Force Base has a high proportion of administrative workers and nearly 60 percent of the Hispanics found among all the closing bases. McClelland has many technical workers and a high representation of Asians.

These base profiles suggest several issues that the Department of Defense must consider in its outplacement efforts. The first is how to successfully outplace employees who have high service tenure but are not yet eligible for retirement. Related but not identical to this concern are the potential pipeline problems that may occur for the department as a whole if the low service tenure categories continue to dwindle. The second is whether or not to customize programs for specific occupational groups at different bases (for example, technical employees at McClelland). A third is the probable volume of outplacements at specific bases or specific states. There is also the issue of outplacement in rural versus urban labor markets, not clearly evident from base demographics, but certainly suggested by the location of many of the 52 bases on the closing list. Finally, the timing of base closures is unclear, but it could vary from a few months to five or more years. This is certainly not a comprehensive list of outplacement issues, but it shows the scope of the task facing the department: high-volume, multiple-site closings, over a 5-year period, across occupations, for employees with high service tenure, in rural and urban labor markets.

The workshop model of outplacement presented in Figure 1 at the beginning of this report serves as a guide for this discussion.

ORGANIZATIONAL OUTPLACEMENT

As an organization, the Department of Defense certainly wants results from its outplacement practices like those shown in the figure. Protecting the department's reputation as an employer who cares about its people, controlling the costs of downsizing, and maintaining a capable workforce are all concerns voiced at the workshop. The Department of Defense has under its control (at least partially) many of the outplacement practices recommended to achieve these results: planning, communicating, resources for the transition, customizing, and monitoring.

Outplacement Planning

In his paper, Bush notes, "the foremost downsizing lesson learned from outplacement experience is: downsizing should be planned, be executed, and be over with." This is the ideal, but the Department of Defense, like many organizations, is faced with downsizing that is incremental and drawn out over years. Nonetheless, the advice still applies. To the extent possible, careful planning will allow the department to plan, execute, and be done with it, in phases. Such phased planning must be based on strategic goals and the resulting labor demands. These strategic considerations and related organizational performance goals (cost reductions, increased productivity, technological upgrades, etc.) should be the overriding criteria for decisions about which employees will be outplaced and which will remain. Planners should use caution in using more subjective individual performance ratings in selection decisions. If the majority of employees view these ratings as heavily biased and unfair, they will view the outplacement decisions tied to them as unfair.

Planning will also allow the department to provide the employees who are to be outplaced with advance notice of 60 days or more. Advance notice increases the likelihood that employees will view the outplacement process as fair. However, it is also important that, once notice is given, the department begins encouraging outplacement orientation and encourages employees to enter job search training. According to Leigh, Vinokur, and other participants, early intervention of this sort has been shown to increase the speed of reemployment and the quality of the jobs secured.

Employees who are to stay for the immediate future can be counseled as survivors. If the Department of Defense wants to experiment, one possibility is to implement some form of job search training coupled with workshops on the new employment contract with survivors. This type of outplacement intervention prior to actual downsizing has not been used often or evaluated, but the remarks made by several participants (especially Vinokur and Diamond) suggest its potential value. Moreover, it is consistent with the notion of helping all employees better understand the implications of the new employment contract.

A second aspect of planning discussed during the workshop involves planning buffers for employees who might otherwise be outplaced. The Department of Defense has already implemented some of these buffers (for example, hiring freezes, retirement and separation incentives), but several others could be considered. These include the special leave of absence programs and the idea of an internal, contract talent bank. Examples of both were described by Jackson at AT&T. The contract talent bank (called Resource Link) at AT&T is used to maintain a source of talented people in which the company has already invested. The Department of Defense might consider such programs as part of phased downsizing at closing bases. The contract talent bank concept might also be considered as a way to get new skills into the organizational pipeline despite freezes on permanent hiring.

Outplacement Communications

All the workshop participants from industry deplored the media coverage of outplacement and downsizing. As Messenger remarked, the media can make the best, most carefully constructed outplacement effort look bad. However, everyone also acknowledged the inevitability of media coverage and suggested that the organization must do damage control via well-conceived press releases, conferences, and other public relations efforts. The visibility of the Department of Defense outplacements will certainly require a proactive approach to damage control. Perhaps the most effective means of damage control is communication of accurate information on job prospects and the successes of outplacement programs in helping employees to find good jobs and retrain for new careers. Although this information is important for public consumption, it is also important in helping departing employees maintain their energies for the job search.

Another aspect of outplacement communications emphasized at the workshop was the importance of repeated and multimedia communications concerning termination. For example, the initial downsizing announcement might be followed by group meetings, and then one-on-one interviews with departing employees. The verbal information presented in these meetings needs to be supplemented by written notices in newsletters, e-mail communications, posters, video tapes, and so forth.

A third aspect of outplacement communications involves decisions on how to handle the time between the announcement of impending terminations and the actual date of termination. Several industry participants noted that their organizations encouraged people to think that their job is getting a job during this period. This means encouraging people to use career centers and begin the process of financial planning, emotional counseling, and career counseling and training. In some cases, for example at AT&T, people who qualified were invited to find temporary jobs within the organization. Diamond (Right Associates) emphasized that this period is part of the overall process of organizational change and downsizing. Managing downsizing must be part of a broader effort to communicate and educate about the changing employment contract; all individuals must think about their employability as well as their employment.

The most critical aspect of outplacement communications is the termination interview. All the speakers emphasized the importance of training the managers responsible for such interviews and providing trained counselors as backup in case an interview goes badly. Managers need to be given the tools and the coaching to conduct what, at its very best, is a difficult interview. Communicating with the survivors is also important, if only to let them know that counseling is available to them through an employee assistance program. The ways in which downsizing and outplacement are communicated to employees have a significant effect on employee perceptions about organizational fairness. These perceptions can influence the motivation and self-esteem of survivors and departing employees.

Resourcing the Transition Center

Although resources must obviously be allocated to all outplacement practices, the workshop discussions focused on the resources needed for transition centers. The basic idea of a transition center is that of a facility, preferably located outside the organization, which offers orientation, counseling, training, and other services that people need to pursue their next move—more training, another job in their field, a new career, self-employment, or retirement. The workshop participants discussed two types of transition centers. The first, described by Ryan, Diamond, Jackson, and Messenger, is a free-standing, off-site facility, rented or owned by the organization. This facility was staffed by experts, either from the company or from a consulting firm, who managed traffic through the center, provided testing and assessment, ran workshops to develop job search skills, and conducted career counseling. These centers were physically well equipped with private workstations, long distance phone services, message services, access to job search databases, and a library of relevant newspapers and books.

The second model for a transition center was described by Papalia and Messenger. In this model, facilities either at local community colleges or somewhere within the organization were rented or allocated as a central location for people to find job leads or get other outplacement information. From this location, people can be directed to counseling, workshops, and testing and assessment sessions in the surrounding community. This model requires more hands-on involvement of the organization in coordinating services and monitoring use of the transition center.

Both types of centers can work. The first requires a higher dollar commitment and is probably more appropriate when there is a high volume of outplacement. The second requires more organizational time but may be more appropriate when outplacement volume is low or occurs in isolated areas in which access to expert consultants is either difficult or very expensive. The second model also features more direct involvement of community members in the outplacement process. This may work to the advantage of both the organization (enhancing its reputation) and the community (providing work for some of its members) in more geographically isolated areas. The Department of Defense must outplace people at bases in both rural and urban areas, with both high and low volume head counts. Thus both models as well as variations on each are appropriate for consideration.

Customizing Outplacement

Research and experience dictate that, whenever feasible, counseling, career guidance, training for job search skills, and pursuing networks and job leads should be customized to people's occupational skills and level. Several of the speakers from industry noted that their organizations set up separate transition or career centers for professionals and managers as well as for hourly workers. At a minimum, counseling and job search workshops were tailored to each of these groups. Such customization reflects the differences in occupational skills and associated labor markets, of course, but also differences in financial resources and personal networks and job search skills.

The issue of special outplacement services for those over age 40 or for those with long service was discussed, and reactions to customization for this group were mixed. All the research for this demographic group shows that reemployment is slower and earnings in new jobs do drop from their previous levels. However, Vinokur noted that, in the JOBS workshops, there is some evidence that a mix of younger and older workers tends to keep older workers energized and motivated to continue searching. The Department of Defense will need to pay attention to motivating longer service and older employees to actively engage in outplacement activities and in job search and should expect that this group may require more time than younger, low-service groups to find work alternatives.

The transferability of skills from government service to private industry is another area in which customizing of outplacement efforts will be needed. The combined expertise of the workshop participants emphasized that it is quite feasible; however, they suggested that up-front preparation of trainers and training materials would pay off. Such preparation would focus on translating government descriptions for jobs and skills into the language used by private-sector employers. This language may vary somewhat by location or occupation, and these variations also need to be considered.

Finally, it is important to note that departing employees will differ in the paths they want to pursue. Some may want to retire, some may want to just stop working, some may want to relocate, others to find new careers, and still others to pursue special training or self-employment opportunities. This is true for even a relatively narrow portion of the workforce such as the older, long-service employees. The organization must keep this broader picture in mind and provide some avenues for employees to consider all these options in its outplacement orientations, workshops, and counseling. Ideally, outplacement services should support individuals in finding the right career for themselves for the long term, not just a quick fix job.

Outplacement Monitoring

How effective are outplacement practices in achieving the results the organizations want? The evidence reported by Leigh from policy evaluation studies of publicly funded reemployment programs suggests that job search assistance is a very effective way to help employees get jobs, but the research results on many other types of programs are mixed. The consensus at the workshop was that most organizations do not do a good job of monitoring outplacement activities, making it difficult to assess the effectiveness of outplacement practices. Ryan noted that, in hindsight, GE Aircraft believes more planning about how to measure outplacement would have improved the company's ability to decide what was working and what wasn't. GE Aircraft has started to monitor activities at its transition center to determine the level of use, which approaches are best in securing jobs, and so forth. Diamond reported that some consultants do develop baseline measures of outplacement activities, but, in general, industry benchmarks and other surveys on outplacement activities are scarce. Given their breadth and scope, the Department of Defense outplacement efforts look like a natural laboratory for monitoring and evaluation research.

COMMUNITY AND INDIVIDUAL OUTPLACEMENT

The workshop outplacement model suggests that organizations must keep in mind the results that communities and individuals seek from outplacement and the pressures they face during downsizing. Communities want to maintain area economic vitality, and job development is one way to achieve this. There was a clear consensus in workshop discussions that the organization must work aggressively with the community on job development. For example, Papalia remarked that Smith Corona worked hand-in-hand with the state unemployment services and with a community task force to identify area jobs and help match these with the skills of departing employees. Ryan noted that job development was crucial in getting jobs for GE Aircraft's salaried employees. GE Aircraft hired professional recruiters to do job development. These experts targeted the top 10 hiring companies in the region and aggressively marketed outplaced workers to them. The Department of Defense could pursue similar tactics, including asking high-level department officials to talk to the top executives of the companies surrounding closing bases.

Diamond described the proprietary Right Associates Job Bank, an electronic database incorporating employment opportunities by specific geographic regions, skills, and experiences against which job seekers can match their own skills and geographic preferences. Other outplacement consultants and recruiters often have access to proprietary electronic databases or can teach individuals to use Web site networks for effective job searches. Employer databases and matching programs have been developed by consortia of public sector agencies, universities, and governments. For example, in conjunction with the Department of Labor and the Department of Defense, researchers at the University of Pennsylvania have developed a database that brings together information concerning individual worker histories with information on job openings and their requirements. (This database was designed for use at the closing of the Philadelphia Naval Shipyard and Base; its development and usefulness are described in Vance and Day, 1995.) The Department of Defense could pursue any of these job development tactics, including asking high level Department officials to talk to CEOs of the companies surrounding closing bases.

Communities are also interested in maintaining effective social services for everyone in the area. Downsizing, particularly high-volume downsizing, places heavy demands on already strained social services. Organizations need to coordinate with social service agencies to ease this burden and to ensure that outplaced employees have access. For example, Papalia reported that Smith Corona put together a company-community steering committee to prepare for increased demand. Several participants talked about one-stop shopping at their companies' transition centers. In order to accomplish this, companies have to coordinate with community service representatives, making arrangements (possibly including funding) for them to keep regular hours at the transition centers. Efforts to ease the burdens of outplacement can work both ways. For example, Ryan remarked that GE Aircraft worked with the local unemployment service to make sure that its outplaced workers were either going through the GE job search workshops or the employment service workshops, if they wanted to collect unemployment benefits.

Although not discussed in detail at the workshop, there are a number of examples of coordination among community service providers in order to create jobs and leverage funding and services, many of which have been partially funded by the federal government, especially the Department of Labor. One example is the Center for Commercial Competitiveness in southern New York (now called Workers Enterprise Development). This center was established by the state and the federal Department of Labor in 1992 to create jobs and promote entrepreneurship in areas hard hit by defense cutbacks, corporate downsizing, and economic shifts away from traditional manufacturing. Center programs offer selected unemployed workers training in team building, business development, new manufacturing systems, and product marketing to prepare them for new manufacturing environments. In conjunction with this training, program officials recruited area employers to support internships, specific projects, and entrepreneurial joint ventures offering workers-in-training opportunities for paid learning experiences. The program encountered many of the barriers to reemployment and job creation documented in the paper by Leigh but may provide some insights to the Department of Defense in coordinating community action in areas such as New York's southern tier. (This program is described in Last et al., 1995.) One common finding in all case studies and descriptions of coordinated community efforts to develop jobs and speed up reemployment is the need to coordinate the rules about eligibility and dispersals made by agencies funding training, unemployment assistance, and other forms of social support in order to provide meaningful (and more dignified) assistance to displaced workers.

Most outplaced individuals want to find new jobs or at least get some guidance about where to go next. They also want to minimize the stress and disruption that accompanies job loss. As Bush and Wanberg and Hough report, there is considerable evidence that job loss can exacerbate existing physical ailments or increase the incidence of others. There is also evidence that violent behaviors such as suicide, spousal and child abuse, and workplace violence can increase. Papalia and Messenger emphasize the need to be prepared for illness or violence by having ongoing hospital, mental health, and security support available to the workplace and to career centers during downsizing.

In addition, Messenger notes how important it is that outplacement centers be places where people can go to get on with the job of finding a job. That is, these centers must provide a sense of safety, of structure, of humor and positive social interaction. At the same time, the center staff must insist that people actively search for jobs, emphasizing that everyone can do it and that rejections are part of the process. In addition, center staff need to promote a sense of balance—people have other things going on in their lives and this whole fabric cannot be completely torn apart during a job search. Losing a job is difficult, but it is not fatal. If, to some degree, these messages can be conveyed in all of an organization's outplacement practices, everyone will be, at minimum, a survivor.

REFERENCES

Vance, R., and D. Day
1995 Developing computerized outplacement and counseling programs. In M. London, ed., *Employees, Careers, and Job Creation.* San Francisco: Jossey Bass.

Last, L.R., R.W.E Peterson, J. Rappaport, and C.A. Webb
1995 Creating job opportunities for displaced workers. In M. London, ed., *Employees, Careers, and Job Creation.* San Francisco: Jossey-Bass.

Appendix

Workshop Agenda and Participants

WORKSHOP AGENDA
February 20-21, 1996

9:00 a.m.	Welcome: Diane Disney, Department of Defense Alexandra Wigdor, National Research Council
9:15 - 10:30 a.m.	Panel Presentations: Current Research on Outplacement Duane Leigh, Department of Economics, Washington State University Leaetta Hough, Dunnette Group, St. Paul, Minnesota Gerald Bush, Heller School of Management, Brandeis University Amiram Vinokur, Institute for Social Research, University of Michigan Renae Broderick, Project Manager, National Research Council
10:30 a.m. - 10:45 a.m.	Break

10:45 a.m. - 12:00 p.m.	Panel Presentations continue
12:00 p.m. - 1:00 p.m.	Lunch
1:00 p.m. - 2:30 p.m.	Panel Discussion: "Best Practices" in Outplacement Susan Diamond, Director, Mobil Career Center (Research and Development), Right Associates Ellen Jackson, Director, AT&T Resource Link, AT&T Anne Messenger, Director, Lockheed Martin Employment Transition Center Anthony Papalia, Director of Counseling and Student Development, SUNY Cortland Jack Ryan, Manager of Recruitment and Placement, General Electric Aircraft
2:30 p.m. - 2:45 p.m.	Break
2:45 p.m. - 3:45 p.m.	Panel Discussion continues
3:45 p.m. - 4:00 p.m.	Workshop wrap-up

WORKSHOP PARTICIPANTS

OFFICE OF THE DEPUTY ASSISTANT SECRETARY OF DEFENSE (CIVILIAN PERSONNEL POLICY)

Diane Disney, Deputy Assistant Secretary of Defense (Civilian Personnel Policy)
Melinda Darby, Director for Staffing and Career Development
David Hyde, Director, Congressional and External Relations
Larry Lacy, Chief, Civilian Personnel Policy/Civilian Personnel Management Service Research Office
Lisa Oakley, Labor Economist, Civilian Personnel Policy/Civilian Personnel Management Service Research Office
Sharon Stewart, Civilian Assistance and Re-Employment Division
Ellen Tunstall, Chief, Civilian Assistance and Re-Employment Division

OTHER GOVERNMENT REPRESENTATIVES

Carolyn Becraft, Deputy Assistant Secretary of Defense (Personnel Support, Families and Education)
Charlene Bradley, Assistant Deputy for Civilian Personnel, Office of the Deputy Assistant Secretary of the Air Force (Force Management and Personnel)
Maureen Cronin, Office of Workbased Learning, Department of Labor
Sherry Holliman, Project Manager, Office of Economic Adjustment, Office of Deputy Under Secretary of Defense (Industrial Affairs and Installations)
Grace Kilbane, Administrator, Office of Workbased Learning, Department of Labor
Dorothy Meletzke, Deputy Assistant Secretary of the Navy (Civilian Personnel Policy and Equal Employment Opportunity)
A.L. Papenfus, Director for Personnel and Security, Washington Headquarters Services, Office of the Secretary of Defense

PRIVATE SECTOR AND UNIVERSITY GUESTS

Marc Bendick, Jr., Bendick and Eagen Economic Consultants
Kerry Bunker, Center for Creative Leadership
Gerald Bush, Heller School of Management, Brandeis University
Susan Diamond, Mobil Career Center (Research and Development), Right Associates
Leaetta Hough, Dunnette Group
Ellen Jackson, AT&T Resource Link, AT&T

Duane Leigh, Department of Economics, Washington State University
Stephen Mangum, Department of Management and Human Resources, Ohio State University
Anne Messenger, Lockheed Martin Employment Transition Center
Anthony Papalia, Counseling and Student Development, SUNY Cortland
Jack Ryan, Recruitment and Placement, General Electric Aircraft
Amiram Vinokur, Institute for Social Research, University of Michigan

NATIONAL RESEARCH COUNCIL STAFF

Renae Broderick, Project Manager, Workshop on Issues in Civilian Outplacement Issues
Alexandra Wigdor, Division on Education, Labor, and Human Performance
Carolyn Sax, Division on Education, Labor, and Human Performance